WHEN THINGS GET

CRAZY

WITH YOUR TEEN

The Why, the How,
and What to Do NOW

MICHAEL BRADLEY, Ed.D.

New York   Chicago   San Francisco   Lisbon   London   Madrid   Mexico City
Milan   New Delhi   San Juan   Seoul   Singapore   Sydney   Toronto

The *McGraw·Hill* Companies

Library of Congress Cataloging-in-Publication Data

Bradley, Michael J., 1951–
  When things get crazy with your teen : the why, the how, and what to do now /
by Michael J. Bradley. — 1st ed.
      p.   cm.
  ISBN 978-0-07-154571-6 (alk. paper)
    1. Parent and teenager.   2. Teenagers.   3. Parentting.   I. Title.

  HQ799.15.B727   2008
  649'.125—dc22   2008024963

1 2 3 4 5 6 7 8 9 10 11 12 13 14 15 16 17 18 19 20 21   FGR/FGR   0 9 8

ISBN   978-0-07-154571-6
MHID   0-07-154571-9

Interior design by Monica Baziuk
Illustrations by Ross Bradley

McGraw-Hill books are available at special quantity discounts to use as premiums and sales promotions or for use in corporate training programs. To contact a representative, please visit the Contact Us pages at www.mhprofessional.com.

This book is printed on acid-free paper.

To Hajime Kondo and Steve McWilliams

Though now they smile from another place,
their love still warms us here.

CONTENTS

PREFACE

"You still don't get it," Marc sighed. "If this book is such a good idea, it would have been written long ago. You can't get that specific with teen behavior problems. They're far too complex. Aren't you the guy who's always saying that each kid is a different book? These are not simple physical issues, and, besides, you ain't no Dr. Spock." Marc was my third peer to advise against writing this book, and he made a lot of sense. A psychologist would have to be nuts to think that one book could help families deal with so many issues. Teenagers, their problems, and their families are all about as similar as fingerprints. That complexity is what forces very smart psychologists to write very generalized books. In the game of human behavior, becoming specific often means becoming inaccurate and looking stupid. So why would someone ever try to write one parenting book crammed with nothing but very specific advice?

Because of what happened to me later that week. At the end of one of my teen-parenting seminars I watched a mom roll her eyes in exasperation as I overanswered her question. "That theory stuff is fine," she sighed. "But what should I do about this *tonight—when I get home*? That's what I came here for. I don't have time to do all those things you just said. That theory stuff might help me do a better job with my kid when things calm down—IF he calms down. I need *practical* help for RIGHT NOW. What should I do TONIGHT?"

That must have been the hundredth time I had heard the same thing from a scared, frustrated parent, but this time something clicked. As I listened to that mom, all those rows of excellent parenting books in bookstores flashed before my eyes. I pictured her picking up one after the other (including my own prior ones), frantically flipping through the pages, and angrily mumbling, "But my kid is raging *NOW*. What do I do *NOW*?" With that picture in my head I quickly snapped off three brief things for that mom to try when she got home that night. She smiled a big, tired smile, nodded, and thanked me. She had gotten what she came for. That's when I decided to write this manual.

What drives most parents of adolescents to bookstores and seminars is not scientific curiosity about adolescent development theory. Usually it's more about the algebra text she just hurled through the picture window. Or the bottle of vodka he just hid in his backpack. Often it's about report cards that mimic the last hours of the RMS *Titanic*. Or the bedroom floors from which the cockroaches flee. The desire to learn parenting techniques typically arises from problems, not perfection. People with those "perfect" teenagers scoff at parenting books. The rest of us (the ones with the normal kids) hold a love-hate relationship with those pages. Speaking as a parent, my hate part comes from being forced to read endless passages while trying to sift out the what-to-do-now pieces. Speaking as a psychologist, I intend to fix that.

In this book you'll find little theory and lots of advice—practical, specific, and well-researched advice. This (hopefully) works because I've limited the scope to provide generally accepted strategies for only the *initial intervention* with each of these teen issues, problems that were selected by parent groups as the ones most common to contemporary adolescence. For most of the smaller problems that you'll face with your teen, this is all you'll need. For the biggies, this will help to keep everyone safer until you get the more involved help you'll need.

Think of this manual as a hospital emergency room (ER) and you'll get the idea. Here's where you get minor problems fixed (such as with a few stitches) and major ones stabilized (as with a temporary cast) until you get to see the specialist. At the ER and in this book you find that knowing what *not* to do is at least as important as knowing what to do. If nothing else, you'll learn how to keep minor disagreements from exploding into major disasters. As an airline pilot once explained to me, "You know, there's a lot of similarity between the training for parenting and the training for piloting. It's often not the *problems* that cause crashes. Frequently it's *our bad reactions to the problems* that create the disasters."

And if your particular disaster is a less urgent one, you really should read the last section of this book first: "The Twenty-Minute Guide to the New-Millennium Teen." Those ten quick reading topics can provide all the ingredients you'll need to concoct your own curative recipe for any teen challenge you might encounter.

In closing, allow me to note four things. First, in the interest of readability, I generally alternate gender references from topic to topic. Of course, almost all of these problems strike both sexes with equal opportunity pain. By the way, the attributed quotes you'll find under the topics are the actual words of real kids. The others I just made up. (But I'll bet the farm they've been heard many times.)

Second, I must acknowledge the risks that my friend Marc pointed out. Indeed, these are simple solutions to sometimes complex problems, and some may not work in your particular situation. Just as you need to be your own "first" physician, so must you be your own "first" shrink. Use this information as options to be considered, but apply them or not according to your own expertise and knowledge of your family. And whenever in doubt, get expert help. If we're frequently wondering whether we need some counseling, then we likely do.

Third, I must apologize for repeatedly telling you to stay calm as you get through these issues with your kid, many of which will absolutely enrage you. Being Irish, I can enjoy a good parental firestorm at least as much as the next parent. Unfortunately, the research is overwhelmingly clear that snapping out at best does no good and at worst can do tremendous damage. To paraphrase an Alcoholics Anonymous mantra, *there's no teen problem that a parent rage cannot make worse.* If you take only one thing from this book, take the idea that keeping your cool is at least 50 percent of the cure for any adolescent crisis you'll ever see.

Finally, know that in addition to researching and gathering this wisdom, I've tried out much of it myself with my own kids. It's amazing—a lot of it actually works!

Good luck! And keep your head down.

ACKNOWLEDGMENTS

FIRST, TO ALL of those who've shaped my thoughts, and so shaped this book, the best I can do is say thank you. Thanks to Bonnie Arena, Pete Bradley, Tony Chunn, Joe Ducette, Mattie Gershenfeld, Fred Hanna, Barry Kayes, Terry Longren, Harry Lynn, Father Michael McCarthy, Sandy McWilliams, Father John Riley, Chuck Schrader, Ginny Smith-Dawson, Marc Stein, Gene Stivers, Pat Williams, and Debbie Young.

Second, a huge thanks to all of my team members at McGraw-Hill, folks who seem to thrive on challenge.

Finally, thank you to the folks to whom I owe debts I can never repay. First, to my daughter, Sarah, who is my joy: thank you for all that adult understanding when your 10-year-old face fell a thousand times after hearing me say I had no time to play. Without you, our family would be without life.

To my son, Ross, who is my courage: thanks for taking care of my family when I could not. I cannot tell you how much I love and admire who you are. Without you, our family would be without laughter.

And to my wife, Cindy, who is my vision. Any good that ever springs from my life is all from you. Without you, our family would not be. You are the best person I will ever know. With all my love, I thank you.

PART 1

BODY/APPEARANCE ISSUES

But I **AM** dressed for the wedding!

REMEMBER LOOKING AT your teen when he or she was just born? *Perfect* was likely the word that sang softly in your head. Beautiful skin, soft hair, and a bright face beautifully accentuated with perfect ears and nose. And remember those great outfits you used to dress him up in? You know, those crazy-expensive jumpers that your great-aunt Annalise would bring? He sure looked great. He even smelled great, so sweet after those fun, bonding baths. I hope you took lots of pictures, because you're gonna need 'em. For now before you stands that model of perfection who desperately wants to desecrate many or most of those things that you held so precious. The thought of piercing, tattooing, dyeing, or otherwise mutilating that perfect body is a horror to

1

you. He doesn't even smell so sweet anymore. And where the hell is Aunt Annalise when you really need her?

Welcome to the appearance battles, those "whose body is this" conflicts where parent and child often wage seemingly senseless wars of attrition until the day that both stagger exhausted into the adult years, wondering what the heck happened and why the appearance fights suddenly stopped at the end of twelfth grade. The fact is that those fights are not senseless at all. They're all about *identity*.

Identity formation is job number one for your child's adolescence, a life-defining process by which she tries to discover who she is by trying on a thousand "hats" (styles, interests, beliefs) to see what fits and what doesn't. Some examples seem obviously important, such as her developing values, morals, life goals, and codes of conduct. But the body battles often get overlooked and underestimated by us parents. For those changes are prized symbols, battle flags marking this critical teenage process. For example, acquiring purple hair can become a safari of critical learning into the jungles of prejudice and irrational fear, those places where someone's interior worth gets judged by her exterior appearance. So when your teen fights for her right to have crazy hair, she's also learning about defending the rights of persecuted minorities to be different.

Your kid will move through this identity process in stages, each with its own critical pieces of learning. These will soon come together to assemble the healthy, happy, and hardworking young adult that your crazy teen is about to become (believe it or not). Each of these stages also has its own set of markers or flags that appear on the surface of your child in the form of clothes, hair colors, piercings, and even (gulp) tattoos. The huge mistake we parents make is blowing these things off as "teen rebellion." If your neighbor gets a tattoo, would you call that "neighbor rebellion"? The fact is that your child is very much like your neighbor, a unique human being with his own values, beliefs, and interests that can vary widely from your own. *Yet you still see him as a good and worthwhile person*—as, you know, that guy with the insane political views who is also the first one at your door whenever you need help.

I hate to be the bearer of scary news, but your child is becoming your neighbor, and she very much needs to do that—not to "rebel" against you, but to find herself, her identity, and to define that thing as separate from you. As parents we all harbor this dark secret of wishing our teens to become smaller extensions of ourselves, of our egos. We want them to think like us, believe as we do, enjoy our music, and look something like us. This is a terrible and debilitating wish. For if our kids succumbed and did those things, they'd be living in our basements when they're forty. *We don't want that.* But the price we must pay now for their independence then is to scratch our heads, sigh, and find the grace to honor these scary appearance changes in our kids for what they truly are: the first shoots in the blossoming of our children into young adults.

So try not to wage wars over these appearance issues, but rather roll with them, and even welcome them as signs that you are doing your job of helping your kid to grow up to become a unique human being—albeit a slightly strange-looking one for now. The supreme irony here is that the more we patiently honor these passing styles of our kids, the more they come back to permanently embrace things infinitely more important than our appearances. They come to embrace our values.

The choice is ours.

Body Image, Has a Poor

"Am I gonna end up looking like *you?*"

—ROSS, AUTHOR'S SON, AGE SIX

The What

DO

- Model acceptance of your own body with humor. ("Believe it or not, I mostly feel good about myself, even though I look like *this.*")
- Praise the heck out of your kid's achievements, especially the small ones. Emphasize fitness versus appearance. ("You ran a mile? That's terrific!")
- Empathize with her concerns. Ask if her feelings change from day to day. ("Are there some days where you feel OK about yourself? How are those days different?")

DON'T

- Model obsession with your own appearance.
- Overly praise or criticize her body's appearance.
- Emphasize appearance over fitness. ("You look great. Are you losing weight?")
- Dismiss her concerns. ("That's silly! You're not ugly. You look great!")

The Why

Teens have likely worried about their bodies ever since the invention of reflecting glass. Those endless hours spent frowning in mirrors were always normal to the age and were painful enough on their own. But this generation of adolescents—male and female—is being pummeled culturally like no other about their appearance, being told incessantly that their worth is all about how they look, not about who they are. Consequently, these kids have set records for worrying about their bodies, clothes, and hair from incredibly early ages. Their obsessing over this stuff only gets worse in adolescence. Having parents add their own critical voices to that crescendo can take kids over the edge into hopelessness, self-loathing, and even life-threatening, appearance-related disorders (anorexia, depression, steroid abuse, and so on).

A wonderful antidote for teens struggling with a painful self-image is watching physically imperfect parents who shrug off these crazy cultural trends (such as perfect bodies) and who look instead to more important aspects in people.

The How

Believe it or not, your teen still watches you (although usually sideways) to see how you handle issues to include body image. If you preen endlessly, constantly worry about your appearance, talk twice as much about how a friend looks as about what she is doing, that's what you are programming into your kid. Conversely, if you focus on who people are—their values, their character, and what they do with their lives—that's what your child will emphasize for herself. The key is to say little about appearances and rave endlessly about values and achievement.

At the same time, don't dismiss your teen's body worries. Her culture makes it nearly impossible to be OK with being less than perfect. This is a very tough time to be a teen. Lend an empathic ear to support her fears without judging them. (See "Communication/Empathy," Part 9.)

Remember that, as parents, we still have the greatest impact in our child's life, for better or for worse. (See "Parenting Teenagers," Part 9.) Use that power very wisely. Help your kid learn that we humans only rent these bodies for a relatively short time, and then we move on. Help your kids start to think about where they want to invest their time and effort: into a body that is going to wrinkle and sag no matter what or into a heart that will grow and shine brighter with age.

Clothes, Wears Provocative

"Dad, everybody dresses like this—including my teacher!"

—KATIE, AGE FOURTEEN

Also see introductory text under "Body/Appearance Issues."

The What

DO

- Stay calm.
- Understand why she's dressing that way.
- Connect first; then discuss. ("Honey, I do know that girls are dressing like that, and I know it's time for you to choose your own clothes. Are there other clothing options that might work for us both?")
- Offer incentives. ("I'll go the extra cost for clothes that cover more of you.")
- Share how your own parents went nuts over your clothing choices (back in the sixteenth century).

DON'T

- Go nuts. ("Are you insane? You look like a slut!")
- Issue ultimatums.
- Assume that the clothes imply cheap sex to her.
- Forget how important your clothes were to you (back in the sixteenth century).

■ Just let it go. There is a deeper issue here that must be addressed.

The Why

The fact is that your daughter is likely dressing this way not for the *boys* but for the *girls*. Teens have an overwhelming need to fit in, to look like their peers, as much as they deny this. If the uniform of the day changes to burkas tonight, tomorrow your kid will be a black tent swooshing down the stairs (remember the "grunge" movement?). Today's sexualized culture has created this look, not your kid. She's just caught up in it.

Reacting angrily or sarcastically will just set that style in stone. Your loss of control can transform a passing fashion issue into a battleground for identity and respect. Your rage can push your daughter farther down that path of sexualized clothing and behavior. Your invasive control measures can create the "super-girl syndrome," where she changes into her uniform in the first phone booth out of your eyesight or, worse, goes crazy when she's finally away from you in college.

Use this conflict to address the bigger issue here, namely that girls are being defined in this culture as the sexual property of males and that the clothes are part of this conditioning. (See "Sexuality," Part 9).

The How

Try to stay cool by not seeing the clothes as *you* see them (advertisements for sex) but as she does—the gateway to identity and acceptance. (See "Communication/Empathy," Part 9.) Dad must be the one to actually tell her she's a few stitches away from dressing like a prostitute, since she'll listen more to an ex-boy's perspective than to Mom's. In that talk, first be sure to tell her all the good things about her and support her need and right to make her own choices about things like clothes, just as you did. Then softly talk about the sexualization issue and ask for her opinions on that critical topic.

Look for compromises where you offer to get her other (new and flashier) clothes that can fulfill her needs and calm your fears. Don't pick them out for her, but tell her your preferred coverage ratios and then let her choose.

If push comes to shove, strike the best compromise that you can and don't go to war over this. If you keep your connection to her heart, the clothes won't take her away from you. But be sure that you get her on to something much better than more conservative clothes. Get her into a frame of mind where she starts to think about valuing herself for much more than her sexuality.

Clothes, Wears Weird

"OK, OK! I'LL STOP WEARING THIS WEIRD HAT! By the way, Dad, how did it end up in your old trunk anyhow?"

Also see introductory text under "Body/Appearance Issues."

The What

DO

- Allow almost all choices. (See "Clothes, Wears Provocative.")
- Negotiate increased autonomy for increased responsibility (e.g., your son gets clothes you dislike in exchange for doing more chores or being nicer to his sister).
- Remember what your clothes meant to you as a teen.
- Offer him a basic budget, and allow him to contribute more if he wants pricier items.

- Look to see if the new clothes are part of a bigger pattern of troublesome changes (mood, sleep, attitude, grades, respect). Get help if you see that pattern. (See "Getting Help," Part 9.)

DON'T

- Make fun of your kid's clothes, especially to others.
- Issue ultimatums.
- Assume that his clothes alone mean a thing about his character—they don't.
- Go to war over clothes. Save your ammo for fights about his heart.

The Why

Clothes to teens can be like battle flags to rebels—they're willing to risk a lot for those symbols. Somehow we parents forget that particular adolescent passion (among others) as we age. Jeans and shirts (or the lack thereof) can become powerful symbols of critical adolescent issues such as identity exploration. The trick with teens is to give them as much power and control wherever we can, and a nonlethal issue like clothing is a great place to do that.

Clothes may make the man, but they definitely do *not* make the teen. I've worked with wonderful kids who looked like frightening, chain-bedecked gangsters and with teen heroin dealers wearing button-down shirts. Don't place too much value on the cover of any book.

The How

Your kid is growing up and needs to be making his own decisions as often as possible, even (or especially) the ones that differentiate him from you. But be sure to get your end of this bargain, namely teaching him that increased freedom must be purchased with increased responsibility. Let him pick the clothes when he demonstrates that he is mature enough to act responsibly in the ways that really count (values, character, and so on).

In all issues like this, before you talk to your teen, talk with yourself—with that old fourteen-year-old part of you hiding out in the attic next to your dusty electric guitar (with the Jimi Hendrix decal). Remember how you prized adults who accepted you for who you were (clothes and all) even though who you were changed every two months. Also remember how you hated those adults who made fun of who you were. Ask yourself which of those adults had more influence over you on important issues like values and character. Then become that person to your kid.

Fat, Is Concerned About Being

"Tell me the truth. Do I look fat in this?"

—DIBBIE, AGE TWELVE

Also see "Anorexia/Bulimia, Has," Part 6, and "Eats Too Much" and "Eats Very Little," Part 3.

The What

DO

- Ask her how she looks to *her.*
- Support her views as true *for her.* ("It must be tough to hate the way you *think* you look.")
- Describe the "variability" factor in yourself. ("One day I look OK to me, and the next I think I look awful. Does that happen to you? Why do you think that happens?")
- Ask what might help her feel better.

- Reassure her only after she's talked as much as she's willing and only about her *worth*, not her weight. ("I'm so proud of who you are. I'm sorry that this hurts you so much.")
- Answer only after doing all of the above. ("Well, I think you look fine, but my guess is that my answer doesn't help you very much.")
- Get help if you see her obsessing over weight or having unexplained weight loss.

DON'T

- Give blanket assurances. ("Oh, you look great!")
- Critique. ("Well, you sure have gained a few pounds.")
- Discount her distress. ("That's silly. You shouldn't worry so much about appearance.")
- Switch to another topic. ("Well, you know you're the best soccer player on your team.")
- Push her feelings away. ("I'm really sick of hearing you whine about this.")

The Why

Perhaps the greatest pressure on today's teens (particularly girls) is about their weight. Girls are literally dying to become "thin enough." What used to be considered a "normal" body is no longer acceptable in the teen world. Giving blanket assurances to kids who don't feel good about themselves is like painting over rotted wood. Your kid will dismiss your words as forced ("Dad *has* to say that") or ill informed ("What does Mom know about how girls are supposed to look?").

Far better to get them to talk out their feelings, much like vomiting up bad food. That helps them get some perspective on this complex and powerful issue.

The How

Your ear, not your mouth, holds your magic. (See "Communication/Empathy," Part 9.) The overwhelming parental urge is to simply reassure a daughter to "make the monsters go away," but she's too old for that now (sorry). Becoming a quiet, nonjudgmental listener, however, can do wonders.

Only after your teen is finished sharing her feelings should you problem-solve and then only if she wants that. Like us adults, kids usually know *what* to do—it's the *doing* that's the rub. Brainstorm with her to look at how you can get better food into the house and what exercise options exist. Perhaps suggest that the two (or three) of you work together to get everyone a little *healthier*, not thinner. Joint shopping trips (for better foods) and daily walks can be great shared-time opportunities.

Most of all, look for other arenas where she can experience success (sports, music, community service). It's amazing how our minds shrink down our monstrous flaws in the face of achievement.

Hair, Wears Weird

"The bald side will grow back, Dad. Just not sure when the purple side will fade out."

—MARK, AGE SIXTEEN

Also see introductory text under "Body/Appearance Issues."

The What

DO

- Stifle your first response, as in "Are you nuts!?!"
- Remember what your hair meant to you as a teen.

- Negotiate for nonpermanent compromises, such as temporary dyes.
- Offer to trade autonomy (the teen alone picks his hairstyle) for responsibility (doing better at school, helping out at home).
- Honor the teen's drive for individuality. ("Boy, that's certainly different. I wasn't brave enough to be that different when I was your age. I really admire your spunk.")
- Stand up for your son if others make fun of his new look.
- Get help if this is just one of many worrisome changes (scary friends, dropping grades, prolonged bad moods, and so on).

DON'T

- Yell, belittle, or become sarcastic.
- Mock your kid to others.
- Assume that crazy hair makes crazy teens—it doesn't.
- Start a war over a hairstyle.

The Why

Hair choices, like clothes and music, are small but critical paths in your child's journey of figuring out who he is. The tactical fact is that the more you fight his wish for iridescent purple hair, the more incredibly appealing it becomes. Better to use this strategic "loss" to gain more important ground such as his level of achievement and responsibility. Isn't it amazing how purple hair doesn't look nearly so bad on an honors student? It works the same with D students who score Bs in the bargain.

The How

Before you open your old mouth to yell, open your young brain to recall what hair, clothes, and music meant to you as an adolescent. Your teen's request (or demand) is one of many messages from your kid saying that he's growing up, and you'd better deal with it skillfully.

Look to get what you can in exchange for your eyestrain (from the purple hair). It's perfectly fair to request that his request be seen as a sign of his growing up and thus that he needs to display increased responsibilities to earn the increased autonomy.

Finally, you should know that in most cases the more you fight your teen about a new style, the longer it lasts. So if you don't like it, keep quiet.

Hygiene, Has Poor

"Hey Mom, why won't the dog come near me anymore?"

The What

DO

- Understand that in his head, your son is six years old and doesn't need to shower daily.
- Understand that in his head, he's also twenty-six years old and must make up his own mind about everything (including bathing and toothbrushing).
- Surround him with the needed supplies (soap, deodorant, and so on).
- Provide gentle, once-a-day reminders. ("Son, you might want to grab a shower after exercising like that. You're a tad ripe.")
- Patiently await natural consequences from his peers. They teach very well. ("GEEEEEZZZZ, dude! You smell like old onions! PHEW!")
- Offer incentives to build hygiene habits.
- Monitor for extreme cases that continue beyond a few weeks or occur along with other symptoms. (See "Depression, May Have," Part 3.) Get help ASAP for this.

- Belittle, badger, or demean him.
- Get hooked into a "you can't make me" battle, since you really can't make him anyway. ("OK, son. I guess you're old enough to decide about hygiene.")
- Let the oily hair become all you see. Your wonderful child is still under that greasy mop.
- Ignore this if it continues beyond a few months, even without other symptoms. See a helper. (See "Getting Help," Part 9.)

The Why

Toothbrushing, bathing, and hair washing are often casualties of your kid's struggle for independence. When he was smaller he pretty much did what you told him because, well, *you told him*. Now that he's larger he often does not do what you told him because, well, *you told him*. He's at an age where he must take the lessons you offer and test them out for himself to see if they're true. This process is a normal and critical (although sometimes odiferous) part of his growth. (See "Adolescent Brain Development" and "Adolescent Psychological Development," Part 9.) The fact that you're reading this section means that he might also be a tad oppositional, the kind of teen who says "black" when you say "white." Getting tough with kids like that can turn short, silly phases into long, nasty battles over power and control. The diplomatic approach can have you running out of hot water from hour-long showers a lot faster.

The How

Calm yourself by trying to reframe that greasy hair and doggy breath as temporary signs that he's growing up and will soon decide that most of your values really do make sense—*if you keep your cool.* If you're feeling like you want to get heavy-handed, know that shortly the world will speak to him most unkindly about his poor hygiene. When that happens, better that he remember you as having offered wise counsel instead of added humiliation. He'll come back for more counsel.

Some parent tricks include bribing and contracting. Bribing involves offering some temporary incentive for bathing so that he gets used to that clean morning or evening feeling (builds a habit) and consequently starts to hate feeling unwashed. (This is an adult value that will build in him on its own.) Contracts include negotiating with him to take on the consequences of his hygiene choices. For example, you might say that it's unfair that others should have to do his overly smelly laundry or that he needs to bear half of his dental/medical costs connected to hygiene-related issues, such as cavities. If you do this, do it dispassionately and not as "stick it to you" retaliation: "Son, since you're old enough to decide about bathing and toothbrushing, I think that you're also old enough to take on the consequences of those decisions. Fair?" When the autonomy hits the wallet, even teenagers are willing to conform a bit more.

Finally, try to remember the time when you went through this kind of phase, when you decided that everything your parents told you was suspect or worse. Picture how you insisted on doing the opposite of what they recommended because, well, *because.* Now recall that humbling moment when you shook your head in amazement and said, "Damn if the old man wasn't right about this. I guess he's smarter than he looks."

Being regarded as smarter than we look might be the zenith of our parental power with our teenagers. That status is well worth tolerating the temporary smell of some old onions.

Piercing, Wants A

"Your ears are pierced, so why can't I pierce my nipples?"

—LORIE, AGE FOURTEEN

Also see introductory text under "Body/Appearance Issues."

The What

DO

- Set a minimum age requirement *before* she "has" to have them (if it's not too late).
- Stay calm (now that it's too late).
- Ask if she has researched the health risks.
- Require a consultation with the physician.
- Have the doc list the piercing areas by relative risk.
- Insist on the least risky area.
- Trade off piercing for increased responsibilities (grades, chores).
- Negotiate the minimum interval before any other piercing can be considered (if any).

DON'T

- Flip out and yell "NO!"
- Say OK right away.
- Accuse her of "following a fad." (Of course she is—so what?)
- Assume that all piercings have equal risks.
- Allow an additional piercing within a short time (six months).
- Assume that a pierced nose indicates pierced character.

The Why

As with clothes and hair, piercings are another of those identity "hats" that mean so little and yet can mean so much. The more angrily these things are resisted by parents, the more attractive (and long-lasting) they become to adolescents. But piercings cross over a health risk line that hair and clothes do not and as such must be handled differently. Beyond the infection, tissue tearing, and tooth risks (from metallic tongues), piercings seem to become strangely addicting to some kids, perhaps giving them a biochemical/emotional payoff similar to cutting. (See "Self-Injures," Part 3.) Multiple piercings is where "harmless" identity exploration (one piercing) starts to get a little risky (several piercings within a short period). The drill here is to maneuver for a little time for you and a lot of thought by her. The time is intended to allow her to move on to a less scary "hat" while awaiting the appointment. The thought part is supposed to help her develop those lifesaving decision-making skills. (See "Decision Making," Part 9.)

The How

Play for time by pointing out from the get-go that piercing one's body is far different from dyeing one's hair and as such requires some thought and planning.

Consulting with the physician can be a sobering experience (ever heard an infected nose piercing described?) and will help her to make a better decision both now and with the ten thousand other decisions coming her way. The doc's war stories may help her safely scale down her plans and take better care of a piercing she eventually gets.

Handled well (calmly) by a parent, a piercing or two will usually do no harm and typically becomes a forgotten passion within a year. But the part that she will never forget is the patient parent who wisely winced, shook his head, and then said, "Well, piercing is a tough one for me, but I'm willing to talk it out. After all, you certainly are a wonderful daughter—even if you are a little crazy."

Tattoo, Wants A

"But I'll *always* want 'THE FLAMING PUKES' etched on my back! And it'll look *great* in a wedding dress!"

The What

DO

- Set this limit early on (*before* your kid can't live without one) and let your kid know.
- Decide quickly (if you didn't set a limit early on) if you'd ever allow this before age eighteen. (Your answer is no, right?)
- Calmly and sorrowfully say no: "I'm sorry, honey, but this one I can't go for. This is a forever decision being made at age fifteen."
- Offer the temporary (henna dye) topical tattoos (they wash off after a few weeks).

DON'T

- Hesitate for one nanosecond—a teen will read that as "maybe" and torture you for three years.
- Blow up and yell.
- Belittle the request as crazy. (Right now it makes all the sense in the world to your daughter; see "Communication/Empathy," Part 9.)
- Think that listening is the same as agreeing and get talked into this. Her anger is valid. Her logic is not. Empathy does *not* require agreement.

The Why

Here's one adolescent identity banner you can't roll with, because a tattoo is a forever flag on a constantly changing creature. You owe your child this protection from herself. She'll hate you for it and know that you are right. I once had a fourteen-year-old client who remained continuously tattoo-obsessed until the eve of his eighteenth birthday when he was finally able to get one without parental permission. The following week he came in unadorned and explained, "Well, when I got to thinking, I realized that if I was allowed to get a 'tat' every time I wanted, on my back right now would be 'GREEN DAY,' 'THE BACKSTREET BOYS,' and, well, 'BARNEY'—you know, the dinosaur."

The How

Ask yourself how you would feel right now if your back sported "TWISTED SISTER" in huge black and red letters. (I apologize if I just hit a nerve. How *did* that look in the backless gown?) And what would you think about the parents who signed the permission slip for that "tat"?

If your teen claims that tats can be zapped right off with a laser, suggest that she do some research to see some pictures of what that procedure looks like (yuck).

As you wait out her "never going to talk to you again" sulk, look for opportunities to expose the flawed logic of tattoos through example. On a trip to the beach, for example, you might nod toward the guy doing his thirteenth beer and say, "You know, I don't think that thing on his chest started out as Chewbacca (from *Star Wars*). That used to be a hula dancer."

PART 2

BEHAVIOR ISSUES

Julie, Honey, You can see your boyfriend tomorrow...
please just calm down pumpkincakes

PARENTING CHILDREN UP to adolescence is much like the regular season in baseball. You know that relaxed, sweetly boring, and seemingly endless time when people routinely leave the games early to get some ice cream, often not knowing the score. "Who cares?" they yawn. "One game doesn't mean much." In the regular season there are always a few heartbreaking losses and some exhilarating wins, but mostly it's a laid-back time in the season of parenthood.

Parenting teenagers is like the play-offs in baseball; you can be on the edge of your seat for every pitch. You sense that one move can end your entire season in a heartbeat. With teens, one word can bring unholy hell to your doorstep.

It's another one of those great tricks of Mother Nature's. We get lulled to sleep raising kids from birth to ten or eleven. It can be hard for a few of us, but relatively speaking, it's easy. We're faster, stronger, and smarter than our opponents, and they actually still think we're cool. They look up to us and mostly do what we ask. And when they don't, we can pick them up and stick them in their rooms for a time-out. Savor those times if you still have them.

If you haven't yet been to those parenting play-offs, beware the cosmic trap that awaits. It comes as a moment when things are going just great with your perfect ten-year-old girl, and you look out your window to see your neighbor on her front lawn being cursed and shrieked at by her thirteen-year-old daughter. You smugly smile and quietly chortle to yourself, "I'll never let *my* daughter talk to *me* like that. That mom must have done a bad parenting job."

Don't go there! Parental karma is a real force in the cosmos. Years later those judgments come back as old memories to cruelly taunt us when our "perfect" daughter is cursing and shrieking at us. I can guarantee that your veteran neighbor won't judge you in return. She'll just sadly shake her head or light a candle or say a prayer for you because she's been to the teen behavior wars, and she knows how tough they can get.

So how do the wars start? Often it's a Fort Sumter moment, an astounding first shot across the walls of your perfect relationship. It can rise up as a sneer at some task request that went smoothly for a decade: "Get ready for church? HA! I'm not going to your stupid church, and *you can't make me!*" That's when a terrible realization suddenly smacks us in the face: "I can't control this creature. She's faster, stronger, and smarter than I am. She doesn't think I'm cool anymore. And I can't pick her up and put her in her room now. What on earth happened?"

What happened is that your little darling is growing up. (See "Adolescent Brain Development" and "Identity," Part 9.) She's *supposed to* become defiant and challenging to some extent. That's her job. Your job is to concede that she may be bigger and faster—*but not smarter unless you concede that ultimate power to her.* You must elevate your game for the play-offs so that your advantage is no longer based on size and speed but on smarts.

Is it possible to manage the problem behaviors with just our wits? Absolutely, but before we get smart about our kids we must first get smart about ourselves by seeing their behavior challenges as simply part of the business side of parenting. *These are not personal attacks on us,* although they can sure seem that way. (See "Parenting Teenagers," Part 9.) Much like insurgents, they're actually confronting the *thing we represent* (authority and control) and not us as people. Once we get that trick down, the strategies that follow are a lot easier to use, and they actually work. Without that mind-set, there are no strategies that will help.

So here you go: some down and dirty dos and don'ts to handle all those small but maddening battles. Remember that they actually symbolize the hidden but critical crusade of a child trying to become an adult. Keep that perspective in your mind so that these small firefights don't evolve into flat-out wars. Remember that nobody wins a war, particularly those wars between parents and teens. One side just loses more than the other.

And in the family wars, it's always the kids who lose the most.

Acts Out (Minor Defiance, Disrespect, Flippancy)

"You can't live with 'em, and you can't beat 'em."

—CHILD PSYCHIATRIST, SPEAKING OF HER OWN TEENAGERS

The What

DO

- Stay calm. (He's the amateur; you're the pro. *Act like one.*)
- Sidestep provocations. ("You're stupid to think that I'll be in by ten.") He's just fishing. Don't let him control you.
- Walk away if you're too angry to keep cool. Nothing good will happen if you stay.
- Confront, but first connect. ("I know it makes you mad that your friends all stay out later, but no one is disrespecting you in this talk. We'll chat later.")
- Look for a compromise if he calms down and speaks respectfully.

DON'T

- Take this personally.
- Get sarcastic or snappy in return (or he'll "own" you).
- Start taking away stuff or grounding on the spot. You can always do that later if need be. (See "Parenting Teenagers," Part 9.)
- Make decisions while you're angry or frustrated. ("Son, I heard what you said. Check with me at dinnertime. I'll have your answer then.")
- *Ever, ever, ever* give in to stop his disrespect or badgering. You'll soon be negotiating with a terrorist.

The Why

Most teens will experiment with acting out to some degree. It is actually a critical part of how children eventually learn to be cooperative. But a strong reaction to your teen's acting out will only make it more likely to happen again. Parental yelling, hitting, pleading, sarcasm, and capitulation all work very well at reinforcing an adolescent brain. It can be irresistible teenage "fun" to control big adults with little words or actions, even (or especially) if the adults go nutso in response. (See "Communication/Empathy," Part 9.) And if that tactic ever works to get a kid what he wants, why on earth would he use any other method?

It's critical to establish two facts in your kid's head with your actions: (1) that his acting crazy will get him nothing from you (including your anger) and (2) that talking respectfully is the way that he can definitely get your attention and possibly your agreement.

The How

Control your emotions by redefining those minor conflicts not as failures but as teaching moments. That arrogant adolescent tone is just an alarm bell telling you that it's time to go to work. Any fool can manage a perfect kid (if there are any). Parents earn their big bucks by teaching real kids who have real problems. You can best shape your kid's behavior (and heart) by working on your own. (See "Parenting Teenagers," Part 9.) For better or worse, our children will be shaped more by the example that we parents set than by any other force in their world. Scary thought, no?

If your kid constantly gets your goat, get some help—for yourself. If you cannot control your emotions, you're in no condition to deal with a teen. If your kid won't quit this game even after you're better at your own for several weeks, get some help for the whole family. (See "Getting Help," Part 9.) Something else might be going on.

Aggressive, Is

"I had a good day at school. I didn't punch nobody."

—SARAH BRADLEY, AUTHOR'S DAUGHTER, AGE FOUR

The What

DO

- Stay calm.
- View his behavior as somehow paying off for him (it gives him power, breaks boredom, compensates for his feeling crummy, and so on).
- Confront, but first connect. ("I worry that something is hurting you, because I don't think you really enjoy hurting others.")
- Ask how his need can be met in better ways (get his own room, more freedom).
- Offer incentives. ("Here's a deal. I'll pay you for each A.M. and each P.M. during which you are respectful to others.")
- Consider more serious causes (depression, anxiety, drug use, bipolar disorders).
- Apologize for your own outbursts.

DON'T

- Deal with your kid when you're furious.
- See this as a terrible moral failing. (He's still a child who's learning how to be a human being.)
- Treat his fist rage with your word rage—that's putting out fires with gasoline.
- "Teach" him what it feels like to get hurt. He already knows.
- Be fooled into thinking he doesn't care what you think about him.
- Accept his aggression as OK or normal ("Boys will be boys"). Too often those boys become aggressive men.

The Why

Many of us parents were raised in a day when a child's aggression was answered with a parent's aggression. That trick only seemed to work a bit back then because (1) the world around our kids was not as in love with aggression and (2) parents were essentially allowed to beat the crap out of their children. Fear can *control* kids, but it won't *teach* them anything except how to instill fear. And it does that very well. (See "Parenting Teenagers," Part 9.)

Mild aggression is normal in young children and early adolescents. That's just nature's way. But in today's culture aggression has become a near religion, an adult-approved philosophy of how to resolve conflict and fulfill needs. (Have you driven your car in heavy traffic recently?) So those normal, "soft" aggressive urges can quickly become hardwired personality traits, particularly if kids see it rushing at them from their parents. The key is to figure out what need your kid is filling by being a jerk to others and then helping him to find better ways of getting what he needs. Those unmet needs and/or pains could be about attention, self-worth, depression, anxiety, power, independence, recognition, and so on. If you don't find and fill that need, not much else will help. Once you've found it, look for win-win ways of getting him what he needs.

Teens are still more influenced by their parents than by anything else. Specifically, they're more influenced by what we *do* than what we *say*. So if we want our kids to stop being aggressive, well, us first. Beating someone to control him is a lose-lose technique masquerading as win-lose. We must model win-win ways of getting what we need.

The How

The first order of business with an aggressive kid is to get our own emotions in hand. (See "Parenting Teenagers," Part 9.) If we're not calm and controlled, we're only guaranteeing encore aggression performances from our children.

I'm not sure I've ever seen a single parenting tool as powerful as an apology in teaching our kids about self-control. Using our own failures to teach our kids success is magical.

In your kid's head, redefine aggression as weakness, not strength: "Wow! A four-year-old kid can make his fourteen-year-old brother so mad that he loses control and gets in trouble? Your little brother must be really smart! It must be painful to get controlled by a little kid like that."

Bribes (I'm sorry, I meant to say "incentives") can be helpful as part of a response package. (See "Bribes/Incentives," Part 9.)

Finally, if the behavior persists, get help fast. (See "Getting Help," Part 9.) Untreated aggressive behavior can eventually get your kid admitted to the graduate school for rage, a scary condition called *conduct disorder*. College is a better alternative, but one your teen won't get to unless he learns to control himself.

Angry, Is Excessively

"I'm not angry! It's just that everything always pisses me off!"

Also see "Aggressive, Is," and "Acts Out (Minor Defiance, Disrespect, Flippancy)."

The What

DO

- Stay calm. (I know it's impossible. Just do the best you can—and see "Apologize, Won't" later in Part 2.)
- Know that occasional "crazy" anger is normal in adolescence. Constant anger is not.
- See your kid's anger as a symptom, not a sin.
- Sidestep nonabusive provocations (they're just diversions from his real issue).

- Focus on your teen's *anger* (feelings), not his *provocation* (behavior). ("I can see you're really angry. What's going on?")
- Temporarily withdraw if your teen won't share. ("OK, I'll just leave you alone for now, but we must chat later. I'm worried about you.")
- Go back when he is calm.
- Accept "*I don't know what's wrong*" as an answer, and then ask him to just say whatever pops into his head.

DON'T

- Take this personally. The odds are it has little to do with you.
- Get angry in response.
- Demand that your teen talk while he's still furious.
- "Punish" unless his words are abusive. (See "Parenting Teenagers," Part 9 and "Curses," later in Part 2.)
- Accept verbal (or physical) abuse.

The Why

Your teen's brain and culture will conspire to create episodes of "crazy" anger, events where he'll go off about things that don't make sense. (See "Adolescent Culture," Part 9.) The fact is that these nonsensical rants *do* somehow make sense . . . to *him*: "Arrrggghhh. I can't believe you didn't buy tuna fish! I told you a zillion times that we need tuna fish! You never listen to me!" If you just interrupt to fire back, you'll have a contest, not a conversation: "How dare you talk to your mother like that! After all I do for you, you say I don't listen to you? Do you know what a pain in the ass you are?"

On the other hand, if you can let your teen vent a bit, the real issue might emerge: "Arrrggghhh. I can't believe you didn't buy tuna fish! I told you a zillion times that we need tuna fish! You never listen to me! No one listens to me! Nobody cares about me!

It's like I'm invisible, like I don't exist! That's why I didn't get invited to Rachel's party."

I hate to be the one to tell you this, dear parent, but you are a stage upon which your child will act out his conflicts. He will unfairly use you as the target for the anger he holds at a million other things. But thank your lucky stars for this. You earned this honor by being someone he can trust, someone mature and loving enough to take his misplaced outrage without abandoning him, someone with whom he can be real. The price you pay for that privilege is to stand firm in the face of the initial blast of fury while you wait for the real pain to tumble out.

But that's a price well worth paying. Remember that in today's world his real pain might be about a minor rejection or a deep depression. So be glad that your teen can get angry in front of you. That's his gift to help you to sort the small splinters from the dangerous daggers.

The How

The idea is to do that Zen warrior thing, to allow his anger to move through you without reacting to it. (Did I mention that parenting teens is very difficult?) The way to pull that off is to stop taking those behaviors personally, to understand that being a teenager in today's world means that your kid is going to be a little crazy now and again. (See "Adolescent Brain Development," "Adolescent Psychological Development," and "Adolescent Culture," all in Part 9.) If you can muster the strength to not flinch or react to his initial outburst, he may begin to calm and start to talk about his real pain.

If your teen is verbally abusive toward you, give him one shot at pulling back. If he continues to attack, withdraw calmly, but firmly make the point that this way of handling anger is not

OK: "Kyle, no one is disrespecting you. If you want an ear, I'm yours all night. If you want a punching bag, I'm leaving. I'll ask you not to go out until we do talk. Let me know when you're ready."

Don't demand an apology as the down payment for communication. That's a bad bargain. When he's quiet, just calmly go back in and try to connect again: "Kyle, what was that about?" Remember that teens often have a hard time regulating their emotions and sharing their feelings. Your teen knows he acted badly, and your patience and grace in the face of his prior provocation will earn you tons of respect with which you can build connections to his heart. Those are priceless lifelines that can save the lives of "crazy" teenagers who often yell about things that seem to make no sense.

WANT TO LEARN MORE?

Get Out of My Life, but First Could You Drive Me and Cheryl to the Mall: A Parent's Guide to the New Teenager, Revised and Updated, by Anthony E. Wolf (Farrar, Straus, and Giroux, 2002)

Staying Connected to Your Teenager: How to Keep Them Talking to You and How to Hear What They're Really Saying, by Michael Riera (Perseus Publishing, 2003)

Yes, Your Teen Is Crazy! Loving Your Kid Without Losing Your Mind, by Michael J. Bradley (Harbor Press, 2005)

Apologize, Won't

"Never ruin an apology with an excuse."

—KIMBERLY JOHNSON

The What

DO

- Know that apologizing is about much more than good manners. It teaches, heals, and grows.
- Teach apology by *doing* it, not *demanding* it.
- Know that a true apology is not conditional.
- Request that your teen apologize to others, but never demand that he apologize to you.
- Suggest written—or e-mailed—apologies if spoken ones seem just too hard.
- Understand that in the middle-school world apologizing *can* feel and look like weakness.

DON'T

- Demand apologies. A forced "sorry" is only that.
- Believe that apologizing makes you look weak.
- Refuse to apologize for your behavior because he provoked yours with his.
- Use the word *but* or the phrase *you must understand*. (Those are excuses, not apologies.)
- Wait for him to apologize to you first. This is not a contest.

The Why

"Apology" might be the most powerful and least understood weapon in our parental arsenal. That's because we parents typically use apologies as things forcefully demanded from our hurtful children as penance. But these work much better as teaching gifts humbly offered to them when they're hurt by us, *especially* after they hurt us first.

A short "sorry" sentence from a parent to a child can teach terribly critical lessons that would put him to sleep if presented as a lecture. Ever try preaching to him about things like owning his behavior, healing pain he's caused in others, wrestling with imperfection, striving to become better? His deflector shields go up after the fifth word. Even if his body hangs around, his brain heads off to Nepal. But a large dad genuinely apologizing to a small teen disables those maddening adolescent defenses because Dad's talking only about his *own* shortcomings, not his child's. The kid's eyes get wide, and he hangs on every word *as long as those words are only about Dad's behaviors and not the son's.*

A true apology is a one-sided affair that speaks only to your side of the fence and does not reference the other. Saying "but" or "you must understand" turns atonements into rationalizations of our bad behavior. Real contrition is an inward-looking process that marks the start of psychological growth and healing from acknowledging our own hurtful behaviors. But these journeys are undertaken only by volunteers, not draftees. An apologetic parent can best inspire these powerful introspections in a child by modeling that behavior right in front of the kid's astonished face.

The How

If your teen has hurt somebody else, it's best to ask that he consider apologizing by asking him to focus on how he thinks the other person *feels* versus what the other person did. Stress that even if he felt justified, "two wrongs don't make a right." If it's a serious offense, perhaps ask that your teen take some time to reflect and write about what he did and ask that he not go out until that process is complete. Present this not as a grounding (punishment) but as an important task that needs to be finished before he can move on to fun things.

The best apology-teaching scenarios are the hardest to do, such as when your kid curses at you and you curse (or slap) back. Our parent minds usually call our actions "discipline" when our parent hearts know it was really retaliation. If you can find the grace to admit that, you've now got a great weapon to get your kid where it really hurts: in his conscience. You do that by apologizing for your actions and not mentioning his: "Son, when I cursed at you tonight, I was wrong to do that. No excuses. I'm the parent, and I'm not supposed to lose my cool like that. I'll try to do better. I'm sorry." And then turn around and leave. Deal with your kid's bad behavior later on, in a separate meeting.

Why separate those talks? Because in that first one you just ambushed him with lessons that a year of Sunday homilies couldn't teach. In five sentences you just taught introspection, owning behavior, humility, respect, wrestling with imperfection, and striving to be better. The trick is that when you talk only about your horrible words, his brain can't resist replaying his own: "Jeez. Here's the old man apologizing to me for blowing up after I called him all those horrible names. I feel like such a schmuck." Feeling like a schmuck is how that growth stuff starts.

If you share my Irish heritage and worry that apologizing makes you look weak, think back to when you were small and what it meant or would have meant if a big, powerful person apologized to you. Think about how you would feel about that person and about the values that person held. Ask yourself if you'd hold those values more or less highly when they come from someone who apologizes. Then you'll realize that you'll never look bigger in the eyes of your child than when you make yourself small by apologizing.

Argues Endlessly

"We can't be done arguing. You haven't given in yet!"

—DAN, AGE SEVENTEEN

The What

DO

- Listen attentively without interrupting (especially to the "crazy" requests).
- Ask for rationales. ("Tell me why you should be allowed to drink beer at fifteen.")
- Restate her argument. ("I hear you saying that all your friends drink, that all their parents are cool with it, and that you're an adult at fifteen. Is that correct?")
- Offer your own views before rendering a decision. ("Here's some info I got online from researching the effects of teen drinking.")
- Decide on a clear and firm answer.
- Insist on thinking time if you need to get clear and firm (or say that her demand for an immediate answer means it's no).
- Give your answer clearly and firmly with your rationale. ("I heard what you said, but I just can't allow something that can hurt you that much. Sorry, but the answer is no.")
- Calmly refuse to revisit your decision or to repeat yourself.
- Calmly leave the room if she badgers or berates you.
- Revisit the badgering behavior after she's calmed down. ("When you berate people like that, you are even less likely to get the next thing you want from them. You'd get more if you stayed calm.")
- Repeat this exact sequence with each of her new requests.

DON'T

- Interrupt until she's said everything she wants.
- Equivocate. If you're not sure, punt (take some time to decide).
- Ever, ever, ever allow her nagging to cause you to cave (change your mind).
- Explode or answer in anger. (Those decisions are often reversed out of guilt.)

The Why

When parents ask why their child badgers endlessly, that question usually implies its own answer: *because that child has learned that badgering gets her what she wants.* And what she wants may surprise you.

Her obvious goal is to get her way. If in the past one hundred requests you have ever caved in to badgering and reversed your decision, then you have taught her brain that its path to success is to torment you until you give her her way. If you do well for ninety-nine incidents, and then collapse on one, you just bought yourself another hundred torture sessions until her brain starts to think that perhaps torture won't work any longer. The more often you've collapsed, the more powerful is her learning and the longer it will take for her to unlearn.

Her less obvious goal is to make you crazy. (She doesn't even realize this.) The fact is that a screaming parent can be neurological "fun" to a teen brain, giving it lots of stimulation. What teen brains hate most of all is *no* stimulation. So giving in to tantrums is very reinforcing. And going nuts in the face of tantrums (with threats, screaming, insults, and/or punishments) is also very reinforcing. What makes that behavior start to stop is to "reward" it with *no* payoffs: no reversals, no drama, and no explosions. Just flat line: boring, quiet responses.

Even when you are sure of your contrary answer, allow your kid to argue her point because this will help her learn the arts of constructive argument and negotiation. If the request is a nonlethal one and is presented calmly and respectfully, reward (reinforce) that behavior by granting the request or some part of it whenever possible. Listen even to the lethal requests, because they give you a magical window of opportunity to get some critical data into that brain when you respond with your rationale ("Well, here's some research that shows how drinking at age fourteen versus twenty-one raises the risks of addiction by 500 percent.")

The How

The key is to control your emotions first, to help your teen eventually control her own. View her ongoing tantrums as if she's trying to quit cigarettes, something that's very hard to do. Expect slow but steady progress where you'll see her badgering declining in intensity and duration (if you can keep your cool). Maintaining a log helps you avoid going insane during her "withdrawal" by charting her progress.

Don't get hooked into threats and counterthreats. If your kid yells "Oh, yeah? What are you gonna do if I just go to that party anyway?" do not respond. Just say one time, "Honey, I'm your parent. I love you and I'm telling you that it's dangerous, and that you can't go. Sorry." Don't issue threats in response to threats since that becomes a game of "chicken." Teens win at chicken every time.

If she does bolt, then calmly implement whatever consequence is appropriate. ("Hello? Police? I'm calling to report a possible teen beer party at. . . .") Your job is to help your teen's brain learn that you say what you mean and mean what you say—*especially* when you've said it only once and very calmly.

Curses

"If my kid didn't curse, I'm not sure I'd know his voice."

—CHERYL, AGE FORTY-SIX

The What

DO

- If needed, wash your own mouth out first.
- Understand that, in the teen world, yesterday's "damn" is today's "f———."
- If you don't curse, calmly tell him that, "as silly as it sounds," you find cursing offensive, and ask him to please stop.
- If you do curse, apologize for modeling that behavior, and suggest that you both need to stop.
- Ask your teen why he thinks people (not him) curse so much these days.
- Ask him how he views adults who curse versus those who don't.
- Ask him how he thinks teachers, recruiters, and employers view teens who curse.
- Note how "cheap and easy" cursing is. ("Don't middle-schoolers do that the most?")
- Ask what the foul language payoff is for him.
- Think about why your child curses (peer influence, power displays, parental shock), and try to address that issue.
- Reward him for each day you hear only the "King's English" from his mouth.

- Suggest a "curse" jar where *any* family member who curses must place a dollar, with the weekly/monthly sum going to the cleanest mouth in the house.
- Get help if the cursing is assaultive in nature. (See "Rages," later in Part 2.)

DON'T

- Accept cursing as "normal" or "OK."
- Argue whether it's "normal" or "OK." (In the teen world it might be.)
- Underestimate the power of parental modeling. (He will likely speak much as you do when he's older, *for better or for worse.*)
- React angrily. (He might curse just to get you pissed—sorry, I mean upset.)

The Why

Cursing has become the verbal punctuation of contemporary adolescent speech. Much as with the dollar, the "F" word just doesn't carry the weight it may have in your day. Understand that the only other people cursing like kids are adult authority figures such as teachers, parents, ministers, and some senators and presidents I could name. So your job is a difficult one since he might not even realize that to many folks his language can be as offensive as the smoke from a trash fire (not a bad metaphor to use). People still make powerful negative judgments about foul-mouthed folks, and you must begin to raise this issue with your sailor-sounding child for his sake, if not yours. Even with the verbal coarsening of our culture, people who curse are perceived by others as being less intelligent, worthwhile, reliable, or trustworthy.

The How

Your first task is to listen . . . *to yourself.* If you practice the art of profanity, your kid will perfect it. Teen swearers with nonswearing parents typically experiment with the sewer language for a tad and then drop it as they move away from the middle-school years. But swearing parents tend to produce kids who swear forever. If the latter sounds like you, take your kid out for coffee and talk about how you think you've done him a disservice, since that dialect will make him look small to others. Say you'd like to elevate your language and perhaps help him do so as well.

The best approach is first to get at his beliefs about cursing by asking him how he sees it, what it does for him, and how hearing it from others affects his views of them. (See "Parenting Teenagers," Part 9.) Then (via the preceding questions) try to redefine cursing as an easy, juvenile, and ordinary thing that slackers and posers tend to do most. (The middle-schooler comment will just kill him.) Be sure to reward the better language days. Beyond all else, control your own reaction to his offensive words since they might be intended mostly to get you yelling, which will buy you lots more cursing. Even if you can't completely stop your kid's profanity now, know that if you model better adjectives and keep your cool, his developing brain cannot resist starting to copy your own better speech in ways that will emerge as he gets older. Pretty f'ng cool, no?

WANT TO LEARN MORE?

Cuss Control: The Complete Book on How to Curb Your Cursing, by James V. O'Connor (iUniverse, Inc., 2006)

Hyperactive, Might Be

"Why do you say I'm hyper you always say I'm hyper did you say I'm hyper nobody else says I'm hyper don't you think I'd know if . . . ?"

The What

DO

- Know that being "hyper" can be one symptom of attention-deficit/hyperactivity disorder (ADHD).
- Take an informal evaluation of your child. Look for problems with focus, poor frustration tolerance, restlessness, and impulsiveness at school, at home, and with friends.
- Get an expert evaluation if in doubt.
- Understand that ADHD is a real disorder and not an "excuse" for willful, lazy, and nasty behavior.
- Know that ADHD occurs more often than ever before.
- Know that ADHD can remain hidden until adolescence.
- Find the patience of Job. The calmer you are, the calmer he'll be.
- Get deaf—sidestep as many verbal provocations as possible.
- Praise like crazy whenever he's attentive, calm, or controlled.
- Use lots of nonverbal direction such as behavior charts and written chore lists.
- Keep him in places where "hyperness" is an asset, such as sports.
- Add fifteen minutes to every interaction (ADHD "time bumpers") to keep your "deadline panic" in check.
- Help your teen see his disorder as a difficult condition, not a character flaw.
- Get family counseling if everyone's unhappy.

- Take your child's behavior personally. (No, he *can't* be like his sister.)
- Let him think that his *disorder* is *him* any more than if he had diabetes.
- Yell at him. Raging at a kid with ADHD is like trying to put out fires with gasoline.
- Use many words or task requests in a row. His brain changes channels all the time.
- Ever give your teen his cousin's ADHD med to "see what happens."

The Why

We don't know the why—why so many kids seem to have ADHD these days (especially the boys)—but the one sure fact is that this disorder is for real, even when we account for overdiagnosing. Many kids can compensate for ADHD as younger students until the academic and developmental demands of adolescence hit.

ADHD is clearly not a voluntary behavior. These teens definitely have brains that don't work as they should. For parents, perhaps the most infuriating example has to do with what looks like defiance. These kids often appear to ignore parental directives. But if the task isn't on a sticky note attached to their nose, it often vanishes from their thoughts. Folks with ADHD frequently describe their brains as TVs being controlled by a remote held by someone else: *the channel keeps changing without warning.* These teens also have poor "brain brakes" to rein in their impulses. They actually will *say* what you *thought* when you were a teen. Scary, no?

Children with ADHD often arrive at adolescence with lots of baggage, including lousy self-esteem, poor academic skills, terrible ability to tolerate frustration, few good friends, class-clown/ bully identities, and so on. This disorder is so challenging that whenever experts are evaluating "criminal" teens, they typically find undiagnosed ADHD lurking underneath those tough exteriors. And in spite of their sneers and jeers, these kids are not happy campers. They suffer a lot.

The How

ADHD is not amateur night in the parenting game. Get expert help to get the treatments and training you'll need to help your kid. In the interim, here are a few suggestions.

Try to get your son into places where he looks more normal and you don't. These include all motion activities such as sports, martial arts, hiking, dancing, biking, and so on. Get a talented tutor who knows how ADHD kids learn best to help with school. Counseling helps a lot by giving your kid a place to talk about his maddening behaviors with someone who won't get mad.

At home, use more written directions than spoken orders. Your words easily get lost in his head, but a well-placed list or chart stays put. Sidestep verbal retorts as much as possible and try not to engage. Just quietly note something like, "Son, no one is disrespecting you," and then withdraw. If he does the task, praise the heck out of him and tell him how much that meant to you.

Most of all, don't let his disorder become his identity. These kids just assume that this is who they are and who they will forever be. You must find that other kid hiding inside, the one who wants to do well. Beneath every bewildering ADHD costume (gangster, clown, or loner) is a sad child who desperately wants to learn to be OK and happy. Your job is to find that person and help him learn how to be free. Tell him twenty-four/seven that his flawed brain chemistry is not flawed character of the heart. You can help a lot by focusing on the good about him and minimizing the bad.

Jackson Browne spoke well for your child when he sang, "Please do not remind me of my failures, for I have not forgotten them." Trust me when I say that a teen with ADHD is painfully aware of his failures.

WANT TO LEARN MORE?

Taking Charge of ADHD: The Complete, Authoritative Guide for Parents, Revised Edition, by Russell A. Barkley (Guilford Press, 2000)

Independence, Demands

"I'll be eighteen in thirty-seven months—you can't tell me what to do!"

The What

DO

- Sidestep the mutinous statements. Your teen is *supposed* to resist your control. (See "Adolescent Psychological Development," Part 9.)
- Agree that she is getting older and should have more freedom.
- Offer more autonomy in exchange for more responsibility. Tell her this is the way of the adult world.
- Quietly note that less autonomy will result from less responsibility. Note that this too is the way of the adult world.
- Allow riskier freedoms with conditions. ("We'll agree to stop the tutoring if you agree that you'll restart if your grades drop after a month.")

- Take this personally. Teenagers are supposed to push for freedom.
- Grant freedoms that could badly hurt your child (dropping out, drug use, and so on).
- Just blow off her demands without listening.
- Just cut her loose. (Believe it or not, total freedom feels like *rejection* to her.)
- *Ever*, not even once, grant autonomy to end her badgering or you'll have just taught her how to get whatever she wants from you.

The Why

Is your teenager in your face, insisting on making her own decisions? Well, congratulations! You've apparently been doing your parenting job well since that's a sign that she's feeling competent, secure, and safe enough to start to solo. Now more than ever your parental mission must be not to control your kid but to teach your child to control herself. (See "Parenting Teenagers," Part 9.) Under that prime directive much is in play when your teen demands more freedom. Your job is to balance out the relative risks against the possible gains in each of those negotiations. Your goal must *not* be to simply avoid any failure but to structure things so that, *win or lose*, your teen learns a lot. This might be the toughest part of parenting, where you see your independence-demanding child headed for a bloody nose (some failure), but you let her go knowing that she'll be so much the wiser for the bleeding that she'll learn how to avoid the next hundred punches to the face. Wisdom ain't cheap, and growth isn't painless.

The How

Try to link your teen's levels of autonomy to her levels of responsibility so that the real power is in her hands, not yours. For example, allow later curfews as long as she makes good drug-avoidant choices. (Alcohol is a drug.) If (when) a drinking incident occurs, temporarily pull back that freedom with the caveat that the freedom will return when she's shown control over that behavior for some time. If she's demanding an AP course at school that you worry she can't handle, consider letting her reach exceed her grasp so that she learns about college-level demands before she hits those beaches. She may withdraw licking her wounds, but perhaps she will also resolve to master the discipline of study with less challenging courses for now so that she's eventually ready for "thirteenth grade." These are all maddeningly complex calls to make with no easy answers, but even if your teen fails, she'll fail knowing that you respected and loved her enough to allow her a shot at something you worried was a bad idea.

WANT TO LEARN MORE?

Get Out of My Life, but First Could You Drive Me and Cheryl to the Mall: A Parent's Guide to the New Teenager, Revised and Updated, by Anthony E. Wolf (Farrar, Straus, and Giroux, 2002)

Uncommon Sense for Parents with Teenagers, Revised, by Michael Riera (Celestial Arts, 2004)

Lies

"Presidents lie all the time. So, like, ground me."

—ERIC, AGE FOURTEEN

The What

DO

- Stay calm. Your anger will provide your teen with an escape from the issue.
- Check the mirror. If your kid sees you lie, you need to clean up your act first.
- "Welcome" his lie. You now have a great teaching opportunity on a critical topic.
- Understand that to a teen brain, lying can make lots of sense.
- Also understand that your teen likely does feel crummy about betraying your trust.
- Know that he's still learning about trust and truthfulness. (See "Adolescent Brain Development," Part 9.)
- Separate your teen's *lying* from the *issue about which he lied* into two different talks.
- Teach about, don't punish for, lying. Say that there is no punishment that repairs broken trust.
- Use a metaphor to teach. ("Son, if your best friend lied to you, would you doubt the next thing he says? And what would that doubt do to your relationship?")
- See a helper if he lies chronically. Something else is up.

DON'T

- Get wounded by the lie. Your teen is an "adult in training," not your spouse.
- View this as a huge moral-ethical failure or character flaw. He's a kid, remember?
- Punish for lying. (But do set a consequence for the thing about which he lied.)

The Why

Before you go nuts over your kid's prevarication (great word, no?), try remembering your own teen fibs. Recall what great sense they made: "My drinking had nothing to do with Mom and would only get her upset. What she doesn't know won't hurt her—or me either." Many adolescent researchers see the lying phase that many teens go through as a normal problem-solving response of their developing brains. Younger teens in particular really don't have the wiring in place to fully comprehend a higher-level value like trust. So view your kid's bald-faced provocation as a sign that it's time to go to work—to *teach*, not to *punish*. Grounding him for a week for lying might tell him that if he *gets caught* lying in the future his "fine" would be a week inside, perhaps a reasonable price to pay for getting drunk at the upcoming prom. *Teaching* instead helps him understand the true cost of betrayal, which is really the loss of connection to another human being.

The How

Break these incidents into their two *very different* parts. Deal with the *issue* piece first: "*Since you broke your brother's CD, you need to replace that for him.*" Then ask him to come up with his own "punishment" for the *lying* part. Gently reject each suggestion and ask him to continue thinking about this problem since groundings, chores, or fines won't help you rely on what he says next. The idea is to have him wrestle with the essence of these issues of truthfulness and trust. When he runs out of ideas, teach by metaphor and/or describe trust as an exquisite stained-glass window, a treasure made up of a thousand small acts of honesty and caring, a priceless work that is easily shattered with one rock, with one thoughtless impulse. Point out that it takes another thousand acts to rebuild trust and that if it's broken too often it sometimes never really gets fixed. Finally, tell your teen that hearing truth from him, *especially difficult truth*, helps you to feel very close to his heart. Then let it go. Will he lie again? Probably, but the repeated lesson will eventually take hold. Remember that your job is not to create a perfect teen but to shape a wise adult.

WANT TO LEARN MORE?

Your Adolescent: Emotional, Behavioral, and Cognitive Development from Early Adolescence Through the Teen Years, by David Pruitt and the American Association of Child and Adolescent Psychiatry (Collins, 2000)

Rages

"People who fly into a rage always make a bad landing."

—WILL ROGERS

The What

DO

- Stay calm. Your restraint can quiet his rage; your yelling can detonate it.
- Mentally impose your kid's two-year-old tantrum face on that fourteen-year-old rage body. (It makes things less scary.)
- Quietly ask that he leave until he gets control of himself.
- If he refuses to leave, calmly leave the area.
- Refuse to discuss the issue that prompted the rage until he's calm.
- If he physically threatens you and/or restrains you, tell him *one time* that you'll call 911 if he continues.

- If he continues to threaten, call 911 without a second warning. *Do not rescind that call even if he calms.* (Otherwise you might be calling again soon.)
- Go back after he is calm to ask what happened and how you can prevent that from ever happening again.
- Be sure to always apologize if you "lost it" as well.
- See a helper if this happens again. (See "Getting Help," Part 9.)

DON'T

- Demand that he leave if he refuses that request. That can become a lose-lose contest.
- Yell, threaten, or push back. Gas doesn't put out fires.
- Run away; just walk. Show him sadness and control, not fear and panic.
- Issue consequences on the spot. (This is the time for containment; the parenting part comes later.)
- Continue to discuss his issue while he's raging. Show him that nothing ever gets decided while people are out of control.
- Think that rage is somehow OK for parents. It's OK for no one.

The Why

Rage is that scary region beyond angry and upset. It takes anger and turns it into a weapon by adding a lack of control along with a terroristic demand that someone witness and/or be the victim of one's fury. *Your response to rage must be very different from your response to anger.* An angry teen is to be listened to while he talks. A raging teen is to be disengaged from until he's calm. His rage-triggering issue is to be dealt with only *after* the rage has been discussed and resolved. If there are physical threats, restraint, or contact, call 911 after one warning and never rescind that call even if he calms down. Tell the dispatcher that your son is out of control and that he's threatening you. *Do this even (and especially) if you are a black belt and twice his size.* The flashing red lights in the driveway are embarrassing, but they convey a powerful statement to your child that rage is never acceptable as a method to achieve an end and that he will never succeed in getting you hooked into that dangerous behavior of using physical force to resolve emotional conflict.

The How

Staying calm in the face of your teen's rage might be the hardest and single most respect-getting interaction you can have with your child. Your staying composed teaches him that he is not in your league in terms of emotional discipline and control, adult skills that he badly needs to master. The first way to stay cool is to paint his old toddler face on his new, teenage body. Understand that what you're really seeing is the same two-year-old tantrum but this time on a large-screen TV with a *great* sound system. Your second trick is to use the "Jedi Mind Control" (*Star Wars*) techniques, which include (1) the more crazily he gestures, the calmer you become, and (2) the louder he yells, the more quietly you speak. ("Son, no one is screaming at you. Please calm down" and "Please leave and then come back when you are calm.") If your kid continues to rage, don't repeat yourself or turn up your volume; just calmly withdraw. (He'll quiet amazingly fast without an audience.)

Why not just scream back? Well, have you ever noticed how hard it is to continue screaming at someone who speaks respectfully? Have you ever noticed how easy it is to scream at someone who's screaming at you? The fact is that calmness is contagious, so contaminate your kid by modeling the behavior you want to see in him.

After the storm passes, go back in to resolve things. The odds are that he's already feeling humiliated and ashamed even if he acts as though he was justified, so go easy. If you raged back, *apologize* for your actions *even if your insanity was only a response to his.* (See "Parenting Teenagers," Part 9.) Then ask what happened and how the two of you can work to keep that from ever happening again. Explain that it's OK to be angry but not to be assaultive, physically or verbally. State that if he wants to hurt with hands, or wound with words, you'll be gone in five seconds, and nothing good will happen. But add that if he wants to share his feelings, *especially his angry ones*, you're his all night, and maybe together you'll find a solution before the sun rises. Which, by the way, it always does, even after the dark night of a scary rage.

Responsibility, Refuses to Accept

"Liberty means responsibility. That's why most men dread it."

—GEORGE BERNARD SHAW

The What

DO

- Sidestep circular arguments about how it's never your teen's fault: "This is what I did that contributed to our fight. Does any small part of this belong to you?"
- Know that the more failure she ducks, the less success she feels.
- Check the mirror. Are your own faults your own, or do you duck as well?
- Know that owning shortcomings is hard for adults and much harder for teens.

- Apologize at every opportunity.
- Hand over decision-making power wherever possible with the caveat, "You decide this alone, and you accept the responsibility alone—deal?"
- Ask questions about how she feels about a mistake and what she learned from it.
- See a helper if this is hurting your teen's life. (See "Getting Help," Part 9.)

DON'T

- Argue pointlessly. ("Yes, it is." "No, it's not." "Yes, it is." "No, it's. . . .")
- Berate, lecture, or "advise" her about her mistakes.
- Demand apologies or admissions of fault. (Only those freely offered count.)
- Use the words *but* or *you must understand* in any apology you offer. (Those are excuses, not apologies.)

The Why

Taking responsibility for oneself is one of those critical kid growth tasks that you want to encourage but in ways that might surprise you. (See "Adolescent Psychological Development," Part 9.) The key is not to *force* but to foster your teen to be responsible by showing her what that looks like. That modeling is best done through parental apologies or disclosures of our own contributions to problems and our resolutions to improve. ("It's partially my fault that you're late for school. I knew that you were exhausted and might fall back to sleep. Next time I'll double-check.") (See "Parenting Teenagers," Part 9.) The encouragement part comes from your resisting your irresistible urge to yell, lecture, or "advise" her when she's screwed something up and instead letting her talk it out, with you mostly being the quiet listener.

The How

Remember that people who are never wrong are usually those who feel too fragile to be *allowed* to be wrong. So yelling, belittling, or even giving unwanted advice makes those fragile folks feel even worse and thus less likely to own their next mistake.

Congratulating your teen on any self-admission of fault helps her feel courageous and confident enough to be imperfect the next time. So if your kid *ever* makes a mistake (just kidding), try using quiet questions instead of angry lectures. If she comes home upset after a terrible fight with a friend, ask: "How do you feel about that?" "What did you learn?" "What would you do differently if you could?" "What would you like to do about this now?" The drill here is for your kid to learn to look inward to evaluate and learn about herself in ways that she never would if you just told her what was wrong with her or told her what to do.

Which, by the way, is the magic of parental apology. In that thirty-second *mea culpa* for blasting her about the messy family room (which was really you venting about your boss being crummy), you will teach your child things that no two-hour sermon ever could—things such as owning our behavior, wrestling with imperfection, striving to do better, and, best of all, having *permission to be imperfect.* ("Honey, when I freaked out today, it was not about the family room. It was about my own frustrations from work. I'm sorry I dumped that all over you. I'm the parent, and I should know how to control that. I'll try to do better.") Without those treasures of insight and self-acceptance, we're doomed to a life of risk avoidance and paralysis. With them, all becomes possible in the world of human endeavor.

WANT TO LEARN MORE?

Uncommon Sense for Parents with Teenagers, by Michael Riera (Celestial Arts, 2004)

Risks, Takes Excessive

"Dad, tell the truth: did you ever go 120 miles an hour?"

—RONNIE, AGE SIXTEEN

The What

■ DO

- Know that some teen risk taking is normal and, like it or not, *desirable.*
- Know that teen risks can be about drugs, sex, or thrill seeking.
- Know that repeated and excessive risk taking is not normal and should be evaluated ASAP. (See "Getting Help," Part 9.)
- Calm yourself down before you talk with "Evel Knievel" (your kid).
- Offer to substitute "safer risky" behaviors that might give him the payoffs he needs.
- See a helper if this continues and/or involves dangerous activities.

■ DON'T

- Go crazy. (You'll drive his behavior underground, where it's much more dangerous.)
- Impose punishments that hurt. Instead, use consequences that teach. (See "Parenting Teenagers," Part 9.)

- Ignore repeated risk taking as "boys will be boys." (They might not become men.)
- Forget the upside of risk-taking behaviors: identity exploration, peer status, skill/confidence/values building, and so on.

The Why

Most experts agree that teens are designed by Mother Nature to take risks. (Does she really hate parents?) Their neurology conspires with their culture to cause them to be attracted to many activities that are the stuff of parental nightmares. (See "Adolescent Brain Development" and "Adolescent Culture," Part 9.) Some kids actually push the behavior envelope as a method of feeling better because almost dying can boost depressed brain chemistry. If you doubt this, some morning when you're feeling down, race your minivan as fast it will go for as long as it takes for the cops to shoot out your tires. If you survive, I'll guarantee that as they handcuff you you'll be many things, but you will not be *depressed*—you will be "WWHHOOOAAA! WOW! WHEW—I'M ALIVE!!" For a moment, that sadness will be gone. Sad teen brains can accidentally discover this biochemical fact and then learn to love near-death experiences for the rush (and temporary mood elevation) that they produce.

When the roof-to-pool jumper is not your own child, it's easier to appreciate how risk taking also serves many critical developmental purposes. Acting crazy can build identity ("Gee, I guess I'm not someone who enjoys racing trains to street crossings."), confidence ("I never thought I could climb that rock without safety ropes."), and even values ("I feel lousy about having ripped off my friend. I'll never do that again."). Of course, that stuff only helps if your kid lives long enough to use it.

The How

So if your teen seems addicted to envelope pushing, hide the car keys and get to a helper fast. That chronic, excessive life gambling suggests that other serious things are going on besides normal teen development. If your teen is only sporadically nuts, help him (via the following questions) understand his behaviors and then build in the "brakes" his brain temporarily lacks to rein in those scary impulses. Ask him insight questions such as "What do you think about what you did?" and "What do you think led you to do that?" and "Are there better ways to get what you're looking for?" and "What would you do the next time?" Don't lecture, judge, or belittle his answers, but just ask questions such as those to help him connect his own thoughts in a way that leads him to better decisions.

Then help him channel those energies into less risky adventure pursuits. If you can find the money, those teen adventure programs are pretty cool. (Ocean kayaking in a dense fog will get your heart pounding.) Rock climbing works well, as do many edgy competitive sports such as boxing, karate, and football. Offer to fund/allow these activities in return for your teen's giving up roof jumping.

Don't seek to eliminate all risks because in the proper dose they can teach so much. But do scale them back to a more reasonable level. As parents of risk-taking teens, we must become the brain wiring they lack until they mature a bit and then start to look at speedometers reading triple digits and say "Mmmmm, maybe I'll slow down to two digits. Three seems a little bit over the top."

WANT TO LEARN MORE?

The Primal Teen: What the New Discoveries About the Teenage Brain Tell Us About Our Kids, by Barbara Strauch (Anchor, 2004)

Why Do They Act That Way? A Survival Guide to the Adolescent Brain for You and Your Teen, by David Walsh (Free Press, 2005)

Yes, Your Teen Is Crazy! Loving Your Kid Without Losing Your Mind, by Michael J. Bradley (Harbor Press, 2003)

Spoiled, Is

"But I want *another* horse!"

The What

DO

- Know that giving her too much can "give" her depression, fear of adulthood, self-loathing, and poor self-confidence.
- Know that the proper dose of frustration and denial (working and waiting for what she wants) makes her stronger, more confident, more resilient, and happier.
- Explain to your spoiled daughter that she no longer qualifies for welfare, that she must now earn her "toys" with grades, chores, and volunteer service.
- Pay her to do meaningful volunteer work to get her out of Disneyworld and into "Realworld" (soup kitchens, shelters, missions, hospitals, and so on).

DON'T

- Criticize your teen for being spoiled—instead, *do something to help her be better.*
- View her being spoiled as a character flaw. (She's just taking advantage as any child would.) Rather, see this behavior as a sad way to live her life.

- Lecture about "back in my day" (the days of dinosaurs are not very relevant to teens).
- Fear hurting her self-esteem by not giving her all the toys that her peers have. (*Earning* her toys will *boost* her self-esteem.)

The Why

Many, perhaps most, of today's financially successful parents are negligently not giving their teens the one gift they need more than any others. That gift is a treasure called *resilience*, but it ain't cheap. It comes only with denied want, long-term (versus immediate) gratification, frustration, anger, and, worst of all for too many parents, conflict. Consequently, we neglect our children (by giving them everything) for the worst and best of reasons. Some of us can't stand the thought that our kids might dislike us, so we cave in to their every toy demand. Others remember our tough times, the difficult struggles that many of us endured to get where we are, and we've sworn that our kids will never know that pain. But our pain and our deprivation were our *gifts*, our sources of strength, discipline, self-reliance, persistence, self-confidence, energy—all those things that comprise that magic called *resilience*. At the other end of the dollars spectrum we see financially limited parents beating themselves up, believing that they are handicapping their children from success because they *can't* give them everything. So are rich kids doomed to drown in excess and poor kids doomed to fail from want? Not at all. The successful kids, rich and poor, are both blessed with parents who know that the real gold lies not in the trophies but in the *struggles* to earn the trophies. To teens, hard-earned, ten-year-old Toyotas bring more happiness than gifted, new BMWs.

The How

If you're mad at your kid because she's spoiled, stop blaming her and look in the mirror for the real culprit. Your teen is only doing what any of us would do if given the opportunity. (Offer me a free Ferrari and see if I say, "No thanks. I'd rather earn this.") So the first step in "spoiling cessation" is to turn our own heads around about what it means to be a truly "giving" parent. Take your teen out for coffee to negotiate a structure within which she can now earn her own toys, but push "work" that sneaks in lessons about struggle, privilege, compassion, tenacity, and a thousand other values. Perhaps offer to put her on salary to volunteer in places where she'll earn those priceless treasures. She will surely complain, but don't be too surprised if her protests are conveyed with a lack of passion that suggests a knowing that you're right.

Love your child enough to hear her whine that none of her friends get treated this badly by their parents. Love your child enough to help her earn what she wants. Give her more by giving her less.

WANT TO LEARN MORE?

Ready or Not, Here Life Comes, by Mel Levine (Simon & Schuster, 2006)

Too Much of a Good Thing: Raising Children of Character in a Permissive Culture, by Dan Kindlon (Miramax, 2003)

Violence, Loves

"My violent games don't make me violent. WHEN YOU DON'T BELIEVE ME IT MAKES ME WANT TO F———NG KILL YOU!"

—JOSH, AGE FOURTEEN

The What

DO

- Know that exposure to screen violence (movies and gaming) *probably* increases aggressive tendencies in many teens.
- Know that exposure to home violence (hitting/screaming from or between parents) *definitely* increases aggressive tendencies in most teens.
- Model nonviolent conflict resolution (no screaming/hitting).
- Negotiate for less violent games whenever possible. But:
- Forbid any games that include sexual violence. (One popular game allows you to beat a prostitute to death—just for, you know, fun.)
- Repeatedly express your concern about and disapproval of glorified violence (especially sexual violence).
- Restrict his access to weapons. (See "Adolescent Brain Development," Part 9.)

DON'T

- Just accept his violent pastimes without engaging them with concern and discussion.
- Forbid all violent games without just cause or he'll "just" go underground with his "cause."
- Assume that your kid will definitely be made violent by games. (Many teens are not affected.)
- Use your own violence (verbal or physical) to combat his.

The Why

A great paradox of contemporary adolescence is that, contrary to the beliefs of parents and teens, theirs is one of the *least* violent generations of adolescents we've ever measured. Except for areas where gangs are growing, today's teens commit fewer violent crimes than kids in your own generation. Nevertheless, these numbers would likely be even better if children were not exposed to real violence in their homes (physical and/or verbal) and virtual violence on their screens (TV/computer). A bigger worry involves the far larger and more frightening number of kids who are victims of sexual violence. Their culture has wedded (pun intended) the concepts of sex and aggression into a dangerous facsimile of what used to be called love and transmits that "fax" with astonishing electronic efficiency via screens and headphones. While sexual violence has always been a tragic part of the human experience, it has never before been so skillfully packaged, promoted, and pounded at a generation of young people. And as we found out with cigarettes, advertising does pay.

The How

Understand that while the culture of violence is powerful, you are even stronger if you arm yourself with great antiviolence weapons and lose the bad ones. (See "Parenting Teenagers," Part 9.) One bad weapon (for which we often reach first) is hurting your kid for being hurtful. (Your words can hurt as much as or more than your fists.) Like some sci-fi alien creature, your teen will simply absorb all the negative energy you can dish out, mix in an additive called *adolescence*, and then blast it back at you and the world. Another lousy antiaggression weapon is simply forbidding all violent-themed games/music. Because of the cultural prevalence of this stuff, that strategy can become a losing tactic, making those things even more attractive and driving the teen's behaviors underground, where you can't get at them.

Your better response options are things that go after your kid's belief systems instead of his hard drives. These include modeling *peaceful* conflict resolution, apologizing for your own temper losses, and praising him like crazy whenever he holds his anger and instead negotiates some conflict. Consider requiring that he be safely exposed to the real consequences of real violence as a condition of playing violent games. (Volunteer at a veterans' hospital, read survivors' journals, and so on.) Other tricks include some well-designed periodic coffee-sharing chats to help him better see his own cultural violence conditioning and perhaps counteract its effects. Pose questions, but don't argue his answers. (Questions are the best way to stick troubling concepts into his head.) Some queries might include:

- "Do you think that violence is glorified in your world?"
- "Have you ever seen what real bullets do to real people?"
- "Do you think that pounding kids with this violence stuff affects them?"
- "Did you know that of nine girls you know and like as friends, three of them have been sexually assaulted—and probably none of them will ever report it because they're ashamed and scared?"

The one thing you should expressly forbid involves anything that "romanticizes" sexual violence. Despite your best efforts, your teen will still get to see that stuff, but your opposition must be unusually firm and attention getting to alert him to the seriousness of this issue. Point out how those things are really about victimizing vulnerable people (usually females) and encouraging powerful predators (usually males) by implying that this insanity is somehow "normal." Ask if, with his African-American friends in mind, he'd think that games about lynching black people were OK. If racial violence repulses him, then quietly ask your son how games about physical and sexual violence somehow became so cool.

WANT TO LEARN MORE?

Violent Video Game Effects on Children and Adolescents: Theory, Research, and Public Policy, by Craig A. Anderson, Douglas A. Gentile, and Katherine E. Buckley (Oxford University Press, 2006)

PART 3

HEALTH ISSUES

HAVE YOU EVER met a parent who didn't worry about his or her teenager's physical and mental health? Neither have I. Worrying is a standard part of the entire parenting game, but our concerns are rarely more intense than in those adolescent years. We fret twenty-four/seven over their food, character, sleep, behavior, exercise, interests, achievement, drug use, judgment, safety—the list goes on and on, and with good reason. Adolescence is the time of the greatest physical and mental stress in their lives—and in ours too! The tremendous changes that occur in the teen body and mind are unmatched in the rest of a human's life cycle. In many ways these changes are not unlike the explosion of growth that occurs around age two. (Does the phrase *terrible twos* ring an unpleasant memory bell?) While these changes might be tough enough on their own, Mother Nature and contemporary culture conspire to add a few twists to make things *really* interesting.

First, besides the disconcerting child-to-adult body morphing ("What happened to my little girl?"), the most sophisticated parts of the mind do their most critical development in the teen years. This is where the real game of raising a human being is played. (See "Adolescent Brain Development" and "Identity," Part 9.) Values, character, philosophies, codes of conduct—all the things we define as our most "human" aspects—do most of their growth in adolescence. A key part of this development is our kids' natural need to disregard (many, most, all) parental directives and instead learn directly about life through trial and error, something also called *experimentation*. They just insist on making up their own minds about most everything, including health issues. ("I just read a study on the Net that says people drive better when they're high.") While this phase makes parents crazy now, it makes our teens smarter later in that they learn for themselves what works and what doesn't. That type of learning might be the most powerful of all.

You could say that their need to be unhealthy is healthy.

But there is a second twist to this parenting-teens gig. This is the first generation of adolescents raised in an electronic world that massively conditions them with potent "advertising" (movies, music, media) of risky sex, deadly drugs, killer diets, and pointless violence. Does that advertising really affect our kids' behavior? The research says, "YES!" Those tiny earphones and small screens convey huge messages to our kids' vulnerable brains, bombarding them with scary philosophies, values, and codes of conduct concerning things small and big. If, after hearing the suggestion in a song that she stay up all night, your daughter does so, she likely won't die from it. If she engages in casual party sex, she might.

You could also say that teens' need to be unhealthy is unhealthy.

So what to do? In general, pick your battles very carefully. Do what you can about the "Code Yellow" concerns (messy rooms, poor hygiene), but don't get crazy. There are many "natural consequences" that will teach your kid far better with one sentence than you ever could with one hundred naggings. ("Jeez, Brian, I'd like to go to the dance with you, but, well, why do you smell like old onions?")

Ratchet up the pressure a tad for the "Code Orange" problems such as chores and grades, but again, don't draw lines in the sand. Save your ammo for the "Code Red" threats from sex, drugs, and rock 'n' roll (violence). That's where the "learning" benefits of experimentation are dwarfed by the risks. Will your kid still experiment in these scary areas? Yes, your kid will (but not my kid, of course). The unpleasant fact is that both of our kids will experiment, but with the Code Red scares we must draw the lines and say that zero tolerance is the rule.

Why so? Will one beer kill your child? No. But have you yet experienced the "Speed Limit" syndrome, where posting fifty-five miles per hour allows sixty-five, and seventy-five enables eighty-five? To your kid that syndrome says that if one beer is OK, then two must be as well. Which leads to four and then, perhaps, to sixteen? Zero is the easiest number to police, and it sends a strong message that even a little sex, drugs, and rock 'n' roll can bring a lot of pain to a young life.

Alcohol and Marijuana, May Have Used

"I was holding this stuff for a friend."

—BRITTANY, AGE SIXTEEN

Also see "Drugs/Alcohol, Uses Excessively," Part 6.

The What

DO

- Cool down before you blow up. (Consider dealing with this tomorrow.)
- Appear to accept your teen's lame excuse even though you used the same lame excuse with *your* parents.
- Use the event as *your* excuse—to chat about drug use. ("Well, since holding your friend's drugs means that you're involved to some degree, we need to get to the coffee shop to talk.")
- Do a Net search about the neurological effects of weed and booze on teen brains. Do this together and chat about what you find. (Look only at credible sources.)
- Know that your teenager's weed is three to nine times more potent than what you may have known.
- Know that weed and booze can be terribly addicting to adolescent brains.
- State that her poor judgment (in "holding drugs for someone," "staying at the beer party," or whatever) means that you must now check her things and monitor her activities for a while.
- Agree to a consequence if this should ever happen again, such as loss of away sleepovers or drug testing to be sure she hasn't become further involved.
- Let her know that this stuff scares the hell out of you.

DON'T

- Deal with this while she is high.
- Call her a liar. (Even though you used the same, lame excuses with your parents.)

- Go crazy with punishments and yelling.
- Go immediately to drug tests or lockdowns.
- Say "How could you do this to me?"
- Just ignore it because "they all do it."

The Why

Alcohol is included here as a drug because it's not only *a* drug but *the* drug. Booze kills more of our children than all other drugs combined. For teens, marijuana is *not* the "safer drug" as many adults see it. In fact, both marijuana and alcohol are particularly vicious and terribly addictive to soft adolescent brains. (See "Adolescent Brain Development," Part 9.) Kids' eyes go wide when I just hand them the research and let them read it for themselves.

Accept her lame explanation about the drugs without question. Getting into a "Yes, you did"/"No, I didn't" shouting match will get you nothing but trouble. Proving that she's a liar will only further humiliate and infuriate her. She probably knows that you know (the truth), and that's good enough for now. Your goal is not to prosecute her but to make her safer.

Using this issue as an opportunity for another heart-to-heart on drugs will get you a lot, particularly if your teen sees your fear and love and not your anger and rage. Loud parental yelling is easy to blow off. Quiet parental terror (at the thought of losing a child to drugs) hits home and makes kids think. Your first job is to *teach*, not control; it's to shape beliefs, not impose pain. (See "Parenting Teenagers," Part 9.) Remember that the safe kid at the beer party is *not* the one who says, "I can't drink—my father will kill me." That just sets up a game of how to drink and hide it from the old man. It's an easy game that you probably played. The safe kid is the one who says, "Um, no thanks. I don't drink." How you get your teen there is by teaching, not hurting.

The How

Drugs (including alcohol) have become so pervasive in your child's world that they seem normal and "no big deal." As of this writing an alarming number of American parents (33 percent) voluntarily provide these materials to their kids and to their kids' friends. Twenty-four percent use them *with their children.* The unfortunate fact is that most of our kids will experiment with drugs before twelfth grade. You must make this into a big deal by responding calmly but firmly to let her know that this is a concern far beyond daily discipline. The goal is to keep her involvement from progressing beyond experimentation.

Right now your demeanor means everything. You simply must be calm just at the very moment that you want to go berserk. Ironically, the softer you speak, the more she'll hear, even though you likely want to speak louder than ever before. You must gain control over yourself, or you'll lose control over your ability to help your kid.

So do as the courts do. Find your kid guilty. ("I found this stash in your closet.") Then tell her that the "sentencing" will occur later. ("I'm too scared and upset to talk now. We'll talk tomorrow.") You'll be a much smarter-sounding parent by then, and your kid will lie awake all night wondering what the heck will happen tomorrow. Be sure to use the word *scared* and not *mad* so that she gets it that this is a really frightening event, not just a curfew violation.

Go to some new place to talk (like that coffee shop) to underscore the importance of the topic. Be sure to consult with your partner to talk out what your mutual responses will be before engaging your kid.

Overall, the strategy is to start with the least invasive intervention and then ratchet up the intrusiveness of each subsequent consequence if further drug uses occur. This allows your kid to always have the option to pull back from scary behavior and rebuild trust with you. Immediately going to drastic consequences ("You're grounded for seventeen years!!!") could provoke a huge blowup where she might do something that makes drug experimentation look tame. Save your heavy ammo for when you might really need it.

Counseling, Refuses

"And what's an aging hippie gonna tell me?"

—COURTNEY, AGE THIRTEEN

The What

DO

- Suggest counseling when things are calm (not during a confrontation).
- Say that the family (not just he) needs help coping with the issues.
- Note that you're sure that *you* do things that make *him* nuts, and counseling might help you guys work stuff out.
- Request that he think about this and not decide right now.
- Agree that if he hates the shrink, you'll find someone he does like.
- Talk about "a few sessions," not endless therapy.
- State that you've never parented him as a teen before, that you're just making it up as you go along, and some expert advice might help.
- If he refuses, offer an incentive to go with you a few times.

- Ask "What are you afraid of?" When he yells "NOTHING," say "Good. Then waste an hour with me, and I'll stop bugging you on this."
- If he won't go back even though he liked the shrink, let him be a bit. Raise the issue again during the calm after the next storm.

DON'T

- Threaten or bully him into counseling.
- Say that he's crazy and needs help.
- Demand an immediate answer (or he'll just say "NO!").
- Let his siblings, relatives, or friends know anything about this idea without his consent.
- Badger or nag.

The Why

Adolescents are by nature resistant to counseling. (See "Adolescent Psychological Development," Part 9.) In the best of times they're supposed to hate having adults in their business. In the worst of times (when they're angry and stressed), forcing them into treatment is a really tough proposition. To your kid, coerced counseling can feel like a terrible loss of precious and rare adolescent autonomy. For counseling to work well, everybody has to want to be there, at least to some extent. So use a few tricks to help your kid feel some control. (See "Getting Help," Part 9.)

The How

First, accept and embrace his resistance to counseling and acknowledge your own: "I feel weird about this too. It sort of feels like I'm saying that I've failed as a parent. But I guess this is what people do when they love each other and want to work things out."

Next, tell your teen that counseling is a place where everyone will be asked to speak freely, honestly, and *equally*. That thought alone can be very appealing and calming to a troubled kid. So communicate that by offering the counseling option from the position of a perplexed parent, not a critical boss: "This is intended to help us both do a better job with each other." He will see that as a sign of respect for his feelings and will be more inclined to go. Otherwise he'll feel as if he's being sent to the principal for a reaming session.

Although it's admittedly controversial, I've found that bribing (offering an incentive) sometimes helps with very resistant kids since it can give them an excuse to get past their fear and/or pride. It can allow the healthy part of them to get to the help that they know they need. A sharp therapist can often forge a connection even with the kid who "came only for the concert tickets." Even the ones who proclaim that they're not returning usually call a week or two later to say they've changed their minds. It appears that bribes help highly resistant kids get past their anticipatory fear of therapy and become comfortable with the process and the therapist. Then, after asserting their autonomy (by saying they held up their part of the bargain and are done), they can feel free to "choose" to attend. It's weird, but it works.

If all else fails, don't nag, but do periodically revisit this option. The secret he's not sharing is that he hates the conflict as well and *he misses you at least as much as you do him*. He's just a lot better at acting angry, cold, and indifferent than you are—*hopefully*. If you're doing that act better than your teen, get to him fast to apologize and to explain that's an act you put on to cover your fear and pain. That's something teens know all about, and hearing you say it about yourself might help your child see it in himself.

Depression, May Have

"I'm *not* depressed. This is just who I am. I am someone who hates to eat, sleep, bathe, and laugh."

The What

DO

- Know that teens don't show depression in the same way as adults.
- Monitor your teen without crowding or spying.
- Know that aggression, drug use, and promiscuity can actually be teen masks for depression.
- Look for weeklong changes in sleep, food, appearance/hygiene, physical complaints, activities, interests, and energy.
- Listen for death-themed thoughts and preoccupations.
- Ask directly and lovingly. ("I'm worried that lately you seem to feel down a lot. What do you think?")
- Calmly ask if your teen is thinking about dying, since depression and suicide are cellmates. ("Have you thought about ending your life?") (See "Suicidal, Is," Part 6.)
- Listen much more than you talk. (See "Communication/Empathy," Part 9.)
- Get the guns and pills out of the house. (Assume that a depressed teen might become suicidal.)
- Always err on the side of safety: *get it checked out!* (See "Getting Help," Part 9.)

DON'T

- Mistake the isolation of sadness ("Just leave me the hell alone!") as normal privacy demands ("This is *my* room!").
- Think anger is only anger; often that's depression in a wrapper.

- Think only adults get *really* depressed. Teens may suffer even more.
- Dismiss real depression as normal for teens—*it's not*!
- Bury her feelings with pep talks. ("Oh, you'll feel better tomorrow.")
- Talk more than you listen.
- Rely on gun locks and safes when there's a depressed teen around.
- Let your brain tell you that she's OK when your heart says she's not.

The Why

Teenaged depression is a very serious problem that has exploded over the past few decades along with teen suicide. About 20 percent of our teens suffer with clinical depression before graduation, with the girls suffering more often than the boys. The early-adolescent years seem to be the worst teen times, hitting kids with terrible stresses just at the time when they're least equipped to respond. (See "Adolescent Culture" and "Adolescent Brain Development," Part 9.) As antidepressants have been used more, those rates have fallen a bit. As the meds are used less (because of fear that some medicines induce suicide), those numbers go back up. So treatment is a scary and complex issue that requires expert guidance. The killer myth is that it's normal and thus somehow OK for teens to be depressed. Younger adolescents do have mood swings where they're up one hour and down the next, but those are like Caribbean storms that appear out of nowhere and then move on quickly. When that rain hangs in for days, it's time for the parent to hang out with the child. ("Let's get a coffee.") When a storm of sadness moves in for a week, it's time to see an expert. Will that be a waste of time and money? Likely yes, and that's just fine since terrible things *can and often do* happen quickly when depression hits. Also, get the guns and excess pills out of the house. Keep your kid off my list of children who are no longer around because they got to the guns that Dad swore only he could unlock and to the pills that Mom forgot she had.

The How

Some depression is likely unavoidable because there is a strong genetic component to this disorder. Some results from life stress. Most likely occurs as a combination effect ("genes and jerks" as my old teacher would say). Regardless of the cause, the best treatment starts on the trip home from the hospital on the day your adolescent entered this world. Building a strong, respect-based relationship with your kid both reduces avoidable depression and provides constant access so you can quickly see what's happening. (See "Parenting Teenagers," Part 9.) It gets tricky trying to sort out what are normal privacy issues ("Stay out of my room when I'm on the phone!") and what might be the withdrawal and isolation of depression ("Just leave me the hell alone!"). So having a preexisting close connection with your kid helps a lot in sorting that out. If you don't have that connection, ask for a sit-down at the coffee shop to chat. (Bribe the teen to go if you must; see "Communication/Empathy," Part 9.) If she won't talk, you talk—about depression being like asthma, that it's a "chemical imbalance" and not a character flaw or weakness. If applicable, talk about your own or a loved one's bouts with depression and how it can be like falling into a well and not being able to get out. Don't be reluctant to raise the "S" word (*suicide*). Asking about suicide only *reduces* the odds of that horror and does not "put it in her mind" as too many parents believe. If your teen admits to having a wish, a plan, and the means to leave this world, get to the hospital immediately. If she's not suicidal but still refuses help, ask that the two of you monitor things for a week and that she agree to go to counseling if she still feels lousy. Don't hesitate to grease her palm with a twenty if you must. When she's fallen into that well of depression, do whatever it takes to get her a lifeline, since she may not be able to see that she's sinking.

WANT TO LEARN MORE?

Understanding Teenage Depression: A Guide to Diagnosis, Treatment, and Management, by Maureen Empfield and Nicholas Bakalar (Holt Paperbacks, 2001)

Drinking, Has Been

"Whyyssyou ol-olwaze fink I'z [buurrp] drinking?"

Also see "Alcohol and Marijuana, May Have Used" earlier in Part 3 and "Drugs/Alcohol, Uses Excessively," Part 6.

The What

DO

- Calm yourself—right now you need to be a physician first, parent second.
- Check your kid's level of intoxication. If his speech and gait are substantially affected, or if you can't arouse him, *get him to the hospital.*
- Multiply the teen's drink count: if he says "four beers," that might mean sixteen *shots.*
- Consider keeping a breath alcohol analyzer in the house.
- Monitor him for the next several hours for possible *increasing* intoxication, labored/irregular breathing, vomiting, and so on. If you see any of these, *get your kid to the hospital.*

- Know that teens recover from even near-fatal alcohol over-doses faster than adults: *you might be seeing only the tip of this iceberg.*
- Get a substance abuse evaluation if this repeats.
- If your teen is only slightly intoxicated, have the "trial" tonight and the "sentencing" tomorrow. ("I can see that you've been drinking. We'll talk tomorrow.") See "Alcohol and Marijuana, May Have Used" earlier in Part 3. If you have any doubts about his safety, get him checked at the hospital.

DON'T

- Go crazy, as appealing as that seems right now.
- Try to handle this issue when he's high and you're furious, such as now.
- Assume that he'll "sleep it off." He might never wake up.
- Leave him unmonitored while he's impaired.
- Assume that he's taken only the type and amount of drug(s) to which he admits.
- Wave this off as a rite of passage. That's a trip your teen might not finish.

The Why

Today's teenagers more often drink to get drunk, a level of intoxication that is actually a dangerous overdose for an adolescent. They do not have the adult level of impulse control or adult levels of experience to know when to say when, a lousy deterrent even for many adults. (See "Adolescent Brain Development," Part 9.) Their soft brains suffer specific, measurable damage even from small amounts of booze and tend to get wired for addiction much more easily than adult brains. Yet, thanks to their adolescent metabolism, the next day these dangerously overdosed kids can look great, showing no signs of the massive hangover that you or

I would have. That amazing teen physiology can take an alcohol-poisoned fourteen-year-old and twelve hours later produce a star soccer player who never felt better. That blessing turns out to be a curse because this deludes kids into thinking that a .35 blood alcohol level (which can kill) is no big deal and deludes parents into believing that Junior tossed back just one or two last night. Keeping a breath alcohol analyzer in any house with an adolescent makes sense given today's teen world.

Booze appears in most teen stories of sexual assault, sexual disease, pregnancies, and suicide. If that's not enough to get your attention here, know that the purveyors of booze have killed more teenagers than all the other pushers *combined*. And it's not just by way of drinking and driving. One easy way of killing a drunken teenager is to let him "sleep it off." Some have ingested so much that they stop breathing in the middle of the night. Others vomit in their "sleep" (better described as an *induced coma*) and choke to death. The pukers who survive often inhale their vomit into their lungs and develop a nasty form of pneumonia.

I paint these lovely images to shock you out of the insanely common complacency that adolescent alcohol use is somehow OK. I am continually stunned by parents who would rush their kid to the hospital if they learned that he took a handful of pills but who roll him into bed when he comes home incoherently drunk. Both instances warrant a trip to the ER. Write *OVERDOSE* on the chart and on your brain.

Will that 2:00 A.M. ride be a waste of time? Hopefully, yes—and that makes it a great use of time since it might impress upon your kid that he wasn't partied out—he was *poisoned*.

The How

To keep your cool, repeat your mission statement one hundred times: *to teach*. (See "Parenting Teenagers," Part 9.) Smacking him around for barfing ten purple passions all over your white carpets will do nothing about his next overdose except perhaps hasten it. You are competing with a culture that wants to hurt your child, and using fear won't win your race. Knowledge and love will, but those are tools better used the next day, after your kid wakes up.

So tomorrow, ask him what he learned. If he believably says that he won't do this again ("It was stupid and horrible—kids were fighting, puking, and . . ."), put a consequence in place for the *next* event. ("I believe you intend not to do this again. But what if it does happen? Can we agree that would show us that you're not ready for the freedom of away sleepovers for a while?") Then insist that both of you do a Web search on the effects of alcohol on adolescents and then share that research over coffee. (You'll need the double espresso.) Your focus must be on getting at your kid's *beliefs* about what alcohol is and what it does and not just controlling his behavior. If he seems intent on repeating his poisoning, use consequences designed to erect safety fences around your child, but not punishments designed to hurt him. (See "Parenting Teenagers," Part 9.) Keep those fences in place until his judgment and control improve.

If this drug use continues (alcohol is not just *a* drug; it is *the* drug), get help sooner rather than later. The longer you wink at this behavior, the tougher it will be to treat. And the deadlier it will be to your kid.

Eats Too Much

"In all those fast-food commercials, I've never seen a fat person. But all I see in those restaurants are, you know, fat kids—like me."

—MELINDA, AGE FOURTEEN

The What

DO

- Gently ask if your child worries about her weight and whether you can help.
- See the doc to rule out possible medical causes.
- Monitor for bulimia if your teen's weight stays constant even though she eats like a horse. (See "Anorexia/Bulimia, Has," Part 6.)
- Skip the chips. Stock only healthy foods at home.
- Know that sudden weight gain is normal in early adolescence.
- Model and focus on *fitness*, not *thinness*.
- Get the family (not just her) on a fitness/healthy eating plan.
- Back off if she fights you on food.
- Talk ten times more about what's great about her than about what could be improved.

DON'T

- Just ignore the issue. Obesity (now or in the future) is a serious health threat.
- Ever, ever, ever let your teen think that your love and approval are connected with her weight.
- Nag or criticize.
- Allow your kid to see a scale more than once a week.
- Forget that there is a wonderful person inside that body. Don't let her forget either. The world will tell her otherwise— *every day.*

The Why

Weight issues among young folk are nearly epidemic and worsening as you read. The reasons are many but can be summarized by the fact that so many kids hardly move a muscle anymore except to open the cabinet where the junk food is stored. Are they lazy louts? No, they're just like we were, responding to the culture around them. Their culture tells them to eat fat, look lean, and sit in front of screens all day. That's hard to do.

So don't judge your kid from your own childhood experience. In your day, you had to put some effort into becoming obese. Today your child has to work a lot harder just to *avoid* it. Our parental nagging or criticism only adds pounds of sadness and self-loathing to a spirit already sagging under the terrible weight of hopelessness.

Food is another "win the battle/lose the war" scenario for parents. You don't want your child ever thinking that your love can be gained through her pounds being lost. Thoughts like those can help minor and temporary weight struggles explode into lifelong and life-threatening disorders.

The How

Just about every expert agrees that the best weight-loss/weight-control program is, you guessed it, diet and exercise. Don't you hate hearing that? Well, so does your kid. Nevertheless, the science says that the safest, healthiest, and most long-lasting results come from that slow and boring approach of gently altering your lifestyle in ways that you can maintain for the rest of your days as habits. But the agonizingly slow pace of that best remedy doesn't have enough sex appeal for today's adolescent. So be like Houdini and help your kid to do the impossible by disguising it.

If you talk skillfully about lots of healthy things other than your teen's weight, you can help her manage that weight by not obsessing about it. For example, try stressing fitness and nutrition as goals for the whole family, not just for the "problem" kid. We all run farther when we run together and when we're having fun. So perhaps make this a game with "team" (family) payoffs for combined goals achieved: "We each run fifty 'family' miles, eat fifty fitness meals, and we all win a fifty-inch family TV."

Most important, be sure that your child feels, *really, really feels*, that you think she's great no matter how much or how little of her there is. Don't *assume* (as way too many of us do) that your kid feels loved. *Knowing* and *feeling* are two very different things. Stay focused on what's truly important about her—her achievements, her heart, and her character—and tell her about those wonderful parts *every day*. Hearing it can help someone like herself enough to think about carrot sticks. I guarantee that if she's heavy, the world is telling her every day that she's worthless. Wouldn't that make you think about Twinkies?

WANT TO LEARN MORE?

"I'm, Like, So Fat!" Helping Your Teen Make Healthy Choices in a Weight-Obsessed World, by Dianne Neumark-Sztainer (Guilford, 2007)

Eats Very Little

"I had another huge lunch at school today, so. . . ."

—NICKY, AGE FOURTEEN

Also see "Anorexia/Bulimia, Has," Part 6.

The What

DO

- Gently ask your teen if she's trying to eat less.
- Offer to help plan a safe, reasonable diet. Suggest seeing a nutritionist.
- Stress and model fitness, not thinness. ("I really need to get back on the treadmill" versus "I really need to lose ten pounds.")

- Stress and model balanced nutrition, not "carb" obsession.
- Make food fun. Research, shop for, and cook "weird/new" healthy meals together.
- Celebrate and praise *achievement*, not *appearance*. Needlessly losing weight is *not* an achievement.
- Monitor her without being intrusive.
- Know that the best time to beat an eating disorder is *before* it fully takes hold, so don't delay on this one.
- Watch for indications of anorexia such as exercising obsessively, not eating with others, losing 10 percent of body weight, and ceasing menstruation. Get immediate help if you see these signs.

DON'T

- Repeatedly talk about her weight, except when she raises the topic. Then don't talk—just listen. (See "Communication/ Empathy," Part 9.)
- Fight or nag about her eating patterns.
- Think that your kid can "never be too thin." She can.

The Why

Your kid lives in a culture that estimates the worth of people by their size. Everyone knows that thin folks are much better people because they're, well, you know . . . thin, right!? Because of this craziness, our kids are weight obsessed at insanely early ages. And the more controlling and demanding you get about her food issues, the worse those food issues can become. Your demands that your kid eat more (or less) can morph into terrible scenarios where she feels as if your love and approval are linked to whether she eats (and looks) the way you want. This leads to food and weight becoming wars for approval or control, and your teen's battle plans might include anorexia and/or bulimia. A scary number of anorexic kids trace the start of their self-starvation to a single "you're fat" comment from a parent or relative.

Teens tend to think in extremes. When they decide to lose weight, they sometimes stop eating almost entirely (a terrible method that never works). Help your child think about food in terms of *moderation*, not starvation, and *fitness*, not fatness.

The How

Your role is to help her put weight in its place and see that it's one aspect of a person, one that is much less important than many others. There are two ways you can do this. One is to listen when she talks about the terrible dilemma of living in a world where she is programmed to eat fattening foods (by the commercials) and then tortured if she eats them. Don't try to fix that (you can't), but do offer an open ear (and a closed mouth) for her frustration. A second help strategy is to talk about this weird but powerful cultural view of weight and worthiness, to help her see it for what it is, and then be less wounded by it. Ask your teen to consider whether thin people are indeed the best and why—and who it is that says that.

Perhaps the best help you can provide is to subtly refocus her change goals from fatness to fitness by defining true achievement in terms of *distance added* instead of *weight subtracted*. Praise the heck out of her fitness, not her thinness. The most powerful way you can teach that healthy philosophy is to practice it, not preach it.

Know that in today's world some form of weight concern is almost inevitable and that in the end only your child will decide how she will respond. Your goal is to minimize her stress to keep these worries from growing into full-blown disorders. Your calm, supportive demeanor can carry the day. Your criticism can lose it.

Fears, Has Excessive

"Your bed is just more comfortable than mine."

—JEREMY, AGE THIRTEEN

The What

DO

- Know that fear can be disguised as anger, risk taking, and drug use.
- Monitor your teen for unusual fears lasting several months.
- Spend as much "hangout" time as possible with him and listen well to his concerns. (See "Communication/Empathy," Part 9.)
- Listen for signs of bullying or social exclusion. (He may be too ashamed to tell you.)
- Throw out his energy drinks and Starbucks card. (Too much caffeine can brew worry into panic.)
- Offer your teen bribes to try something that he'd like to do but fears trying. (See "Bribes/Incentives," Part 9.)
- Praise your teen like crazy when he tries something in spite of his worries.
- Know that many teens live with hidden anxiety disorders.
- Push hard to get help if these things persist. (See "Getting Help," Part 9.)

DON'T

- Mock or discount his fears. ("Oh, that's silly. It's easy to talk to girls.")
- Think that having an "easy" teen life can insulate him from fear.
- Try to shame or force him into challenging his fears.
- Compare your teen with others. ("Your brother had no problems joining activities.")

- Ever let him think that you'll love him less if he won't do more.
- Hesitate for one minute to find him a helper if he asks for one.

The Why

If there is one universal experience of adolescence, it's most likely anxiety. Contrary to that weird and eternal myth, teen years are usually not the best years for most folks, because many teens worry all the time. They never seem to have the right hair, body, friends, dates, grades, batting average—the list goes on and on. If that weren't bad enough, many kids struggle with genetically based anxiety that makes them feel crummy no matter how good a life you provide.

Scared kids need love and support, not drill sergeants. Terrorizing a kid into confronting one fear won't help him confront others on his own ("I didn't do this—you made me"), and it could backfire into a full-blown panic attack. Teenagers need to be able to talk about their fears *especially* when those fears are illogical. Illogical fears can be far worse than the rational ones since logic is powerless over them. But the more kids can talk about their fears, the more the logical part of their brain can gain power over the emotional part (where those illogical fears rule the roost). But kids won't share anything with anyone who sneers at their fears.

The How

A great way to frame these struggles in your kid's head is to talk about how everybody has an adult (logical) part and a child (emotional) part. Speak about how at age four we are all convinced that there *are* monsters in the closet no matter how many times Mommy opens that door to show us otherwise.

The same is true with adolescent fear. Tell your kid that fear is a normal and healthy part of who we are but that we must learn to decide when to listen to our fearful child voice and when to listen to our adult voice and do what it says *even if the fear voice never agrees and never shuts up*. So when your teen is facing a fear (such as asking a girl to the prom), ask what his child voice is telling him to do and why and what his adult voice is telling him to do and why. Then ask which voice is smarter and which he thinks he should follow.

Offer incentives for doing things that will help your teen overcome his fears (such as participating in school activities or adventure programs, visiting relatives on his own, and so on). Each success experience lowers the volume of that fearful voice and ups your kid's trust in his adult voice. Standing up to our fears happens to be one of the great secrets of a confident life.

Beyond all else, love your teenager. Really, really love him with hugs and hangout time and "You're wonderful because . . ." talks that never mention his fears. Right now he needs to be reminded of all that is good and strong about him since he might never feel more helpless or hopeless than when he's confronting that terrified four-year-old within him.

Grief, Struggles With

"Nothing's the same since Dad died."

—JON, AGE TWELVE

The What

DO

- Stay very close to your teen for at least six months.
- Know that the toughest time usually starts months after the loss.

- Allow (not force) her to talk as much as she's willing. (See "Communication/Empathy," Part 9.)
- Share good memories and funny stories about her lost loved one.
- Share your own sadness and tears but in a measured and controlled manner.
- Ask if there's some way she would like to mark or celebrate the loved one's life.
- Accept her way of grieving, whatever that way is.
- Allow her to sleep in your room for a while if she wishes.
- Watch for red flags of depression, anger, school problems, drug use, excessive death talk, and nightmares. If you see these signs, get help ASAP. (See "Getting Help," Part 9.)
- Keep your child emotionally connected with family and friends.
- Accept her anger at the lost one for dying. ("Dad was just stupid for dying on us.")
- See if any teen grief groups are offered in your community. (Her school should know.)

DON'T

- Lean or dump your own pain on your kid.
- Just leave her alone—though you should try not to crowd her. Seek a balance of alone/together time that works for your child.
- Insist that your teen grieve in any certain way. ("Why don't you ever cry?")
- Believe that this event didn't affect her, even if she shows no pain.
- Hate your teen for hating the person lost.

The Why

Death is a very strange concept for teens. So many seem so pre-occupied with it (in their music and movies), and yet they seem so stunned when faced with the real deal. Because they are only in the process of becoming adults, their reactions can seem very strange to parents. (See "Adolescent Brain Development," Part 9.) The most severe grief usually occurs some months after the loss, just when bystanders think the hard part is over.

Teens' reactions to loss can be all over the place in many ways. Some will cry a lot. Others won't shed a tear. Some will feel abandoned and hate the deceased one for dying ("I can't believe Mom left us like that.") and then hate themselves for hating their lost loved one. Some will try to act like nothing has happened, because having lost someone (especially a parent) makes you so different from your friends. Some will have no idea how they feel, and that alone can make them feel awful. Others will decide that all attachments are dangerous, so they'll start to avoid anyone who really loves them. Each kid must find her own way of dealing with the loss, but with some soft, wise oversight from her parents.

The How

This is one (of many) of those make-it-up-as-you-go-along parenting situations where you must study your child to see how to best help her, since each will grieve differently. The key is to stay close enough to see what's going on, but not so close that she needs to run away. Schedule times to hang out every day. (Late at night usually works worst for exhausted parents but best for troubled teens.) Her talking and your listening are again the best medicine. In her opened-ended, "nonsensical" ramblings you'll hear her heart telling you what she needs, whether that's more closeness or more aloneness. After hearing her ramblings, suggest some options to help her. Some kids may need to get their schedules back to normal ASAP to feel some sense of control. Others may want time off to construct memorials or celebrations (scrapbooks, tree plantings, biographies, and so on).

Before you try to help your kid with her grief, check out your own. As devastated as you might be right now, you must convey a sense of "this really sucks, but we'll be OK." If you can't do this, get some help for yourself yesterday. Find a caring helper upon whom to dump all of your own despair. Your teen can barely keep herself going. She can't be expected to carry your pain as well. You must be in control enough to project an air of *calm* sadness and loss, not hysteria and fear. No matter how grown-up she appears, she's still more a child than an adult, and she'll key her reaction off yours. So as hard as this might be for you right now, get ahold of your emotions before you take on your child's.

Be superhuman. Be a parent.

WANT TO LEARN MORE?

Guiding Your Child Through Grief, by James P. Emswiler and Mary Ann Emswiler (Bantam, 2000)

Medication, Refuses to Take Psychotropic

"If I can't use weed, why should I take this?"

—BONNIE, AGE SIXTEEN

The What

DO

- Know that many kids hate taking medications, and beyond that, most teens hate being told what to do.
- Know that, in the end, you really can't force your teen to swallow a pill. The medication can work only if he *agrees* to try it.
- Listen quietly to your teen's objections without interrupting. (See "Communication/Empathy," Part 9.)
- Acknowledge that medications can have side effects.
- Suggest a trial to see if the medication helps. Say that he can always stop it if he wishes (with the prescriber's guidance).
- Get a helper (therapist) to tackle this issue with your teen if you hit an impasse.
- Do request that he leave this as a future option even if he refuses for now.

DON'T

- Underestimate how hard this might be for your kid.
- Promise that the drug will be miraculous or that it won't have any side effects.
- Contaminate his medication decision with parent anger or power/control issues. ("You'll take it because I said so!")
- Ask for an immediate answer. Let your teen think a bit.
- Assume that he'd love to feel better.

The Why

Taking a psychotropic (mental health) medication is or should be a scary decision even for an adult. Wouldn't you flinch a bit at the thought of putting a powerful chemical into your body, one that will mess with your essence, your "soul" if you will? For your kid, it's even harder since he's also wrestling with issues of power, control, and autonomy. He's at an age where he rightfully wants to feel that he is in charge, not you. He's programmed by Mother Nature to fight controlling influences, be they parents or pills. He even might feel more comfortable with feeling awful if that's who he believes he truly is. Our human fear of change is legendary for keeping us stuck in bad places. Just like us adults, teens will often choose "lousy and familiar" over "possibly better but unknown." Yes, he may sometimes choose to use illegal, powerful chemicals, but the operative word there is *choose*, versus have prescribed (read *forced*). In other words, it's all about control.

The How

So do the judo thing and use the momentum of his control needs against him. Present the medication as providing him with *more* power and control, not less. Say that while street drugs *change* who he is, prescribed medications *help him be whoever he wants* by giving him the same choices as other kids. Use my asthma medication metaphor with him. A person with asthma can't run. The asthma medication can *allow* him to run but doesn't *make* him run. It simply allows him to run if he wants. The pill allows him to be whoever he chooses to be. Suggest that the legal medications can *increase* his power, control, and autonomy.

As a compromise, suggest a trial run of a medication with both of you keeping a log of observations to see if it helps. The medication effects are often very gradual and can take so long to appear that a written record works much better than retrospective human impressions.

Do not promise miracles and do prepare your teenager for possible side effects (as the prescriber should have), but note that often these are temporary. The unsettling fact is that many of these medications do nothing as frequently as they help, and when they do help, the effects are often subtle. ("I don't feel quite so crummy so much.") Beyond that, some kids have to endure a long and extremely frustrating process of trial and error to find the "right" medicine (or mix of medicines) for them, sometimes experiencing offputting side effects along the way.

If push comes to shove, stop pushing and start asking your teen to please consider revisiting this option in the future if he is still struggling then. Affirm his reservations and support his decision to refuse medication for now, but suggest that he monitor how he does fighting his issue without the medication. Your respectful "concession" now can open the door for a better decision later. A shoving match now can eliminate the medicine option for decades to come.

Menstruation, First

"Mom, how much does a sex-change operation cost?"

—BRIANNA, AGE ELEVEN

The What

DO

- Know that this represents a huge and scary change in your daughter's life.
- Know that she will model her reaction to this change after your own.
- Know that first menstruations can occur at much earlier ages than in the past.
- Speak many times in advance of her first period about what to expect.

- Be positive in these talks. Describe menstruation as a very special thing unique to girls.
- Be calmly realistic about symptoms (cramping, bleeding, pimples, moods).
- Respect her wishes about who should know about her first period (perhaps not Dad or siblings).
- Have a family or mother/daughter *celebration* of her first menses as being the milestone that it is.
- Monitor and get help for possible problems: premenstrual syndrome, dysmenorrhea (very painful cramping), or no period by age fifteen. Know that having no periods by age sixteen or seventeen can suggest excessive exercising or anorexia.

DON'T

- Let your daughter be "surprised" by her first period. (That can be terribly traumatic.)
- Be negative, even jokingly. ("Oh, I see that you've gotten your 'curse.'")
- Announce her period to *anyone* without her permission.

The Why

That first menstruation can be the "best of times" or the "worst of times" for your girl depending on how well prepared she is and how you react. Start these preparations very early since girls are starting to have periods at very young ages for reasons we don't understand. One theory holds that the now widespread increased body fat might trigger early menarche (some even at eight or nine years, although most start in early adolescence). Most girls have powerfully conflicted feelings about their first periods since this represents such a huge departure from their prior lives. They are clearly "not one of the boys" anymore, and that can feel like a terrible loss unless you help your daughter turn it into a special distinction that only females can share. Point out to her that the fact that she menstruates does not stop her from doing anything that boys do unless she allows it. Understand that she may feel very weird about this whole business for perhaps six months, and then it should begin to normalize—for her.

But we parents can get very weird about this as well, since many of us grieve this event as the loss of our little girl (particularly if she is the baby of the family). Dads in particular often stop the old tickling, hugging, and wrestling since their little girl is now officially a sexual creature. Those can be devastating reactions that can connect menstruation with loss of love and approval in your girl's already reeling head.

The How

The key to preparing your daughter is to frequently reference menstruation at *prepuberty ages* as an upcoming event in her life. Speak realistically but calmly about what to expect and encourage her to ask as many questions as possible. Acknowledge that there are upsides and downsides, but try to emphasize the special nature of this event as a somewhat scary but also wonderful milestone, perhaps like when she started first grade or went off to camp.

With that first event, stay very close to her and listen to her fears and frustrations about her new "symptoms." Respect her wishes for secrecy, but do so with a quiet, congratulatory attitude of welcoming to the preadult world.

After listening supportively, try to tip her conflicted feelings toward an attitude of celebration and ask to mark this transition with some special event (a dinner, perhaps), including whomever she feels comfortable with. As strange as that may sound, research shows a powerful connection between celebrations of these sorts of milestones and reduced adolescent risk behaviors.

Which is why you must master your own weirdness about her newfound sexuality before you start to deal with her. We dads in particular need to make sure that nothing changes in how we love our postmenstrual daughters, knowing that they are closely studying us in ways that will powerfully affect their ultimate choices in life partners. Remember that your little girl is still hiding out in that young woman's body and needs her parents' love now more than ever. If it helps, give yourself a mini-grief session with your partner (away from your daughter), where you take out the pictures and tissues and sniffle about how your beautiful little girl ain't so little anymore. Then turn the page to welcome your wondrous new chapter of watching a child become an adult. Life doesn't get any more real than that. It is critical for you to embrace that joy because your quietly expressed pride in watching your little girl become a young woman can put a wonderful spin on her attitudes and beliefs about her sexuality that will keep her happier and safer for the rest of her life.

If your daughter waves off the hugs, respect her wishes, but keep offering those snuggle sessions every day. Let her know that her growing up in no way changes your feelings toward her. Like that great salesperson, keep selling those physical symbols of your affection since she'll likely be back to buy them again soon.

WANT TO LEARN MORE?

Period: A Girl's Guide, by JoAnn Loulan and Bonnie Worthen (The Book Peddlers, 2001)

Mood Swings, Has

"I HATE MY LIFE! I HATE YOU! THE WORLD SUCKS! By the way, Sarah's goin' out with me now. Is that cool or what?"

The What

DO

- Pretend that your teen has the "teen mood flu"—he's just throwing up feelings, fears, and frustrations.
- Stay calm. Calm is contagious. This is situational/hormonal/neurological—*not personal.*
- Keep sellin' connection when he ain't buyin' connection. ("I've got time for you whenever you want—just let me know when you feel like hanging out. I miss and love you.")
- Remind him of what's good about him *especially* when he's been snappy.
- End crazy arguments by calmly apologizing for your "contribution."
- Monitor for abnormal moodiness (more on this later in this section).

DON'T

- Feed the fire by overreacting (yelling/pleading/sulking back).
- Believe that your kid really wants to be left completely alone.
- Think your teen's adult body has adult controls over its child moods. (See "Adolescent Brain Development," Part 9.)
- Take his crazy behaviors personally.
- Take his crazy words seriously.
- Pull away from him. (He needs you now more than ever.)

The Why

Remember, *teens are not adults*. First, they do not have the wealth of experience that helps adults to (sometimes) maintain their perspective and not overreact. Second, *teen brains are not adult brains*. Their gray matter is going through extensive neurological renovations that temporarily deprive them of the very tools they need to cope with their crazy world. (See "Adolescent Culture," Part 9.) Third, teens get whacked with tremendous on-again/off-again surges of hormones that would easily drive many adults over many edges.

Mix those ingredients together and you've got a guaranteed recipe for periodic mood swings that can knock your socks off. But there are ways to keep those socks on. Research shows that the best antidote for crazy teen moodiness is a close connection with a calm parent or two. Parents who take a breath and find the superhuman strength not to respond in kind to their crazy teens tend to have teens who are much less crazy. But parents who "give as good as they get" get adolescents who can take crazy to new levels.

However, this parenting skill is not for amateurs. Like with good cops, that level of self-control is a learned discipline. It rarely comes naturally.

The How

The first job is to get yourself in hand emotionally. If you're not up to the task, see a counselor quickly. If your moods are dependent on your teenager's moods, well, you don't want that and neither does your kid, although it may not seem that way. For if your adolescent can control your behavior with his words (make you scream or cry or sulk), his brain may not be able to resist the impulse to divert you to that game every time he needs to draw attention away from himself.

Next, be sure that the mood craziness you're confronting is the normal craziness of adolescence and not something more serious. Some indicators of the more serious include extreme moods such as immobilizing depression (see "Depression, May Have," earlier in Part 3) or strange highs where he seems to think in unrealistic or grandiose ways and takes dangerous risks. Escalating patterns of aggression or anger or *any* assault/restraint behavior qualifies as well (raised fists, brandishing weapons, poking, blocking doors, and so on). See these signs and get help—quickly.

If you think you're seeing "normal insanity," check out the commonsense contributing factors that we always forget to check, such as diet and sleep. (Eat junk and cut your sleep in half for a week and see how stable your moods are.)

Don't allow crazy fights. When you know that he knows that you know that none of what he's saying makes sense, just calmly and powerfully withdraw by *apologizing* (see "Apologize, Won't," Part 2), *especially* when you've done nothing worthy of his mood: "I'm sorry I made you so mad by forgetting to buy your cocoa-poofies." This ends the crazy fight diversion and helps him calm down. Even better, it frames his craziness in *his* head and helps him perhaps then see what's really bugging him.

Most of all, work on your connection to your teen. When he's withdrawn and/or angry is exactly when he needs your love and support most of all. He's just tied up in some terrible knot and doesn't know how to get free. Offer unconditional hugs (that he'll reject) and unconditional listening (that he'll reject louder), but don't quit offering. Let him know that you'll respect his desire for privacy but that you love and miss him. Beg, borrow, and steal time with your kid. After a tough connection day, take a brownie up to his bedroom with a small white flag stuck in the middle and ask to share it with him. Lie on his bed next to him and just hang out without referencing his earlier behavior. Model that unconditional love and acceptance that we're always preaching about.

Your rising above your teen's craziness will help him to rise above it as well. Remember, *you are the most powerful influence in your teenager's life*. Repeat that sentence ten thousand times.

WANT TO LEARN MORE?

Staying Connected to Your Teenager: How to Keep Them Talking to You and How to Hear What They're Really Saying, by Michael Riera (Da Capo Press, 2003)

Obsessive-Compulsive Disorder, Might Have

"Doesn't everyone arrange her socks in size, color, and age order?"

The What

DO

- Look for things such as excessive orderliness or cleanliness, repeated checking, and rituals or rules that don't have a purpose.
- Quietly ask about these things in a way that helps her see the disorder.
- Tell her that this can be treated so that she won't *have* to do these things.
- Know that your teen's thoughts and urges sound crazy to you *and to her*, and they're terribly painful and powerful for her.
- Know that she can't *"just stop it!"*
- Give love, not advice.
- Ask if your teen ever thinks of ending her life. (See "Suicidal, Is," Part 6 and "Depression, May Have," Part 3.)
- See a helper ASAP. (See "Getting Help," Part 9.)

DON'T

- Ridicule or discount her symptoms. (You're likely hearing only a few of them.)
- Ever force your teen to stop a ritual.
- Allow her to think that she is going insane or is weak-minded.
- Think this will go away on its own.
- React with shock or disbelief.
- Allow school absence if at all possible.

The Why

Obsessive-compulsive disorder (OCD) is a terrible problem with two parts. **Obsessions** are unwanted, intrusive, and irrational thoughts that repeatedly pop up in a kid's mind. They make her think contradictory things such as, "My hands are horribly contaminated; I must wash them before I contaminate other things even though I don't know what they're contaminated with" or "I may have left the water running, even though I clearly remember turning it off." **Compulsions** are repetitive, excessive, and pointless rituals such as hand washing, counting or checking things, forced praying, cleaning, ordering, and so on. While these acts give some temporary relief from fear and anxiety, a kid with OCD feels that she *must* perform these rituals or something awful will happen. One part of her brain rationally knows that these thoughts are silly, but another part of her brain irrationally believes that they are true. Fear beats logic in the OCD wars. Her trying to ignore these messages is like your trying to ignore a blaring train horn telling you to get off the tracks: if you don't do what the "message" demands, you both will get terribly anxious and unable to think or do anything else. While most people experience occasional obsessive thoughts or compulsive behaviors, OCD is diagnosed when someone experiences this for more than an hour each day, in a way that significantly interferes with her life.

Be sure to ask if your teen ever thinks of suicide. Some of these kids feel so tortured and hopeless that they wish they were not alive to suffer like that.

The How

Your job is to build a trusting relationship with your child where she feels that she could share something this scary and "shameful" with you. Don't hesitate to ask if you think you see evidence of OCD ("Honey, do you *want* to keep your room this clean, or do you feel as if you *have* to?"). If your teen starts to break down and tell you "crazy" thoughts and rituals ("I have to put imaginary bumpers on all sharp corners I see so that no one gets hurt"), *do not overreact.* Your teen is *not* psychotic; she's just unable to resist thoughts that she knows make no sense. She must see you as calm and lovingly concerned just as if she was describing asthma symptoms. Otherwise, she'll just shut up and go underground with her struggle. That's the last thing you want. The longer this disease goes untreated, the tougher it is to treat.

Don't state the obvious concerning your teen's fears: "Oh, that's silly. Planes don't crash because you didn't say ten Hail Marys." She already knows that, but she can't stop herself anyway. Just acknowledge her pain and conflict, and assure her that she must be very strong to have struggled with this. Also tell her that this is a disorder that can be treated. Much as with asthma, the symptoms may not go away completely, but they can improve tremendously to a point where she can live a happy, successful, and normal life.

Never try to forcibly physically or verbally stop your teen from performing a ritual. That experience can be as terrifying and infuriating for her as my forcing you to disregard that blaring train horn and staying on the tracks. You might stop her from one hand washing, but she'll be sure to keep all her other rituals secret so that she won't ever have to get run over by a train again.

Until you get to the expert, do whatever you can to reduce your teen's stress and anxiety, with the exception of letting her bail on school. When a kid begins to bag school out of fear, that fear can grow exponentially with each missed day. If she can't handle algebra class, perhaps get her a temporary pass from that one class, but insist that she stay in school until the expert advises you differently.

Beyond all else, find lots of extra time to chat. Talk first about her painful struggle with the OCD, but then also talk about what she does well, what is special about her, how she is *not* this disorder, and how much she means to you. Remind her constantly that she is not a disordered person but a wonderful person with a crummy disorder. That belief will help her to heal.

WANT TO LEARN MORE?

What to Do When Your Child Has Obsessive-Compulsive Disorder: Strategies and Solutions, by Aureen Pinto Wagner Ph.D. (Lighthouse Press, Inc., 2002)

Perfect, Must Be

"The thing that is really hard, and really amazing, is giving up on being perfect and beginning the work of becoming yourself."

—ANNA QUINDLEN

The What

DO

- Know that perfectionism is painful pathology, not pursuit of excellence.
- Know that a true perfectionist is *never* happy. ("Yeah, I got a full scholarship to Harvard, but I'm still a loser 'cause everyone knows I had to work so much harder than everyone else.")
- Know that this disorder is linked with depression, anxiety and eating disorders, and suicide.
- Know that this starts out looking like great achievement and grows into terrible loss.
- Monitor for symptoms such as seeing only flaws, feeling no pride in accomplishments, excessively criticizing self and/or others, being unable to accept 90 percent in anything, not handing in finished work, and avoiding challenges where perfection is not likely.
- Offer a bribe for "only" a 90 percent effort with a sharing about how he feels being less than perfect.
- Apologize if you've been pushing your teen too hard.

DON'T

- Think that this is how "winners" think.
- Let your pride in his achievements blind you to his illness.
- Ever rank the worth of his accomplishments over the worth of his happiness.
- Underestimate this disorder as a "character trait." This trait can kill.

The Why

Perfectionism in children might be among the least recognized disorders of our time. Instead of treating it as the serious illness it is, we celebrate it and hold up its victims as models for other children to emulate.

Contrary to the myth, perfectionism is *not* a healthy striving for excellence. It's an exhausting, life-energy-depleting pursuit of the impossible. It's a game where you lose if you lose and you *lose if you win*, because you can see only what's wrong with your performance. Healthy achievers who strive for excellence fail all the time because they are always trying to learn new skills, whether their game be sports, school, business, personal character development, or anything else. These are folks who *love playing their games, not just winning the titles.* They value and appreciate their own hard work and can feel pride in good effort *even when they lose.* They know that true achievement means constantly stretching into new challenges where they will fail a lot until they learn a lot. They can accept themselves as always being imperfect and be OK. They can live life as always being imperfect and be happy.

Perfectionists can see only the score, and even if they're up twenty points, they feel like they're losing. Their effort means nothing. Even after a huge win, they can't "absorb" any good feelings, but dismiss that as "yesterday's game" and immediately move on to feeling lousy about themselves. This horrible, grinding cycle eventually causes them to stop trying to achieve difficult and worthwhile things. That day can come in fourth grade or in the last year of medical school or even after decades of "success," but that day is always coming. And during the time they're strong enough to push off that day of reckoning, they fall victim to other related pain such as eating disorders, depression, anxiety, failed relationships, and suicide. They cannot accept themselves as being imperfect and be OK. They cannot live life as being imperfect and be happy.

Research shows that many perfectionists are created by having once been targets of something called *indirect aggression*, a largely female and terrible type of bullying that uses exclusion and gossip instead of threats and beatings. That certainly fits with the wrenching picture of a devastated child who is forced to play a rigged game called *social acceptance* where your child can never become "perfect" enough to win.

The How

If you think you've got a perfectionist on your hands, first see what's in your mirror. While much of perfectionism may be genetic/biochemical or social, a large part can also be related to having overly critical and demanding parents who promote perfectionism as a healthy philosophy and *the* way to get love and approval. If you focus on the 10 percent your teen got wrong instead of praising his effort for the 90 percent he got right, you might be teaching him that life is all about the score and not the effort—that his worth is all about his batting average and not his character. If that doesn't create perfectionism, it sure feeds the fire.

If that parent is the person you see in your mirror, take your perfect child out for a coffee and tell him that *you* are imperfect and that a great example is how you made a mistake in pushing him to be perfect. Even if you haven't been pushing your kid, he likely believes that your (and everyone else's) love and approval are based on his "batting a thousand" (being perfect). So ask a few questions, such as "Do you feel approved of and accepted by your peers and/or family?" and "When do you feel that you've done a really good job?" and "When was the last time you felt happy with yourself?"

Finally, ask "For you, is school a place to learn stuff you don't know or a place to show what you do know to try to look smart?" Don't argue or lecture about his answers; rather just stick these questions in his head to soak for a while. Follow up with him weekly to see if he's able to begin to loosen up. If things don't seem to improve, then his is a situation that requires expert help. (See "Getting Help," Part 9.) Be forewarned that a common problem with perfectionist teens is that they often refuse treatment since *what they see as the key to their success is actually their disorder.* That's a thing they don't want anyone "messing around with" in therapy.

If your teen refuses treatment, shake up his perfection belief by quietly asking logical, performance-based questions, such as "Well, which do you think is more productive: hopelessly trying to do one thing at 100 percent or happily doing five things at 85 percent?" If he's still waving you off, try challenging (or bribing) him to get only a B+ on some task and to then write about how he feels. If he still won't see the shrink, just ask him to continue to think about what you said. His pain and frustration will grow, and your questions will ring in his head.

So plant seeds for future discussions. Say that you worry that he thinks happiness in the game of life comes only with batting a thousand. Tell him that no one, *no one,* has ever batted a thousand, but many have learned that happiness comes with just learning to love to play the game.

WANT TO LEARN MORE?

Perfectionism: What's Bad About Being Too Good, by Miriam Adderholdt and Jan Goldberg (Free Spirit Publishing, 1999)
What to Do When Good Enough Isn't Good Enough: The Real Deal on Perfectionism: A Guide for Kids (What to Do When), by Thomas S. Greenspon (Free Spirit Publishing, 2007)

Self-Esteem, Has Poor

"What's the point of *me* trying out for the swim team?"

—BEN, AGE THIRTEEN

The What

DO

- Know that poor self-esteem (PSE) is epidemic in teen years, especially among younger girls.
- Know that just telling your teen that she's great will not help and might hurt.
- Be sure that your teen hears more positives than negatives about her from you.
- Let her repeatedly talk out her feelings of worthlessness without interrupting or arguing.
- Remind your child about *specific, true* examples of her achievements. ("I was very proud of how hard you worked on that project. Were you?")
- Offer incentives to get your teen past her "what's-the-point-of-trying-out? I'm-a-loser" thinking.
- Watch for sex/drug/risk behaviors that can bring temporary relief and permanent pain.
- Share your own stories of self-loathing. (Remember that mirror-person you loved to hate?)
- See a helper if this doesn't start to get better within a few months. (See "Getting Help," Part 9.)

DON'T

- Discount or argue your teen's feelings. ("That's silly—you're better than all of those kids.")

- Lavish her with hollow/false praise. ("You're fantastic no matter what you do.")
- Think that simply telling her how much you love her will fix this. (But tell her anyway—it helps.)
- Mistake PSE for perfectionism (see "Perfect, Must Be," earlier in Part 3) or depression (see "Depression, May Have," earlier in Part 3).

The Why

A good definition of poor self-esteem is a general feeling of worthlessness that keeps your kid from doing what she wants or from enjoying the things she does. Most kids see their self-esteem crash in early adolescence (especially the girls) and then feel it slowly rise through their teen years.

PSE does not get fixed with statements of love and unconditional praise. In her mind, your love for her is no longer directly connected to how she values herself. She believes that you "have to" love her and that as a parent you are blind to the terrible flaws that she and "everybody else" sees in her. Saying "sweet nothings" won't help and can hurt her achievement motivation by making her think there's no sense in trying to do difficult things. For your kid to improve her self-esteem she must take on rewarding challenges, attempting things that she wasn't sure she could do and learning that failing with good effort is not really failing at all—that true failing lies in the not trying.

Helping her change requires that she first see the illogic of her self-prejudice and then take on new challenges *even while she still feels like a loser*. The trick is to help her distrust her "loser" voice and help her brain gather data (take risks) that over time will start to prove to her that she is as worthwhile as anyone *even if she sometimes fails*.

Be patient. Building self-esteem in a teen takes several months or even years of effort. Look for slow but positive trends, not instant miracles, and keep that "slow but steady" change perspective in front of her face. When she's down and ducking a challenge, remind her of her recent accomplishments to help her stretch for the next one.

The How

If your teen is unwilling to talk with you about this, don't take it personally. PSE kids often believe that they are a source of disappointment to even the most supportive and loving parents. If she's suffering in silence, get her to a helper ASAP. (See "Getting Help," Part 9.) She'll talk more easily about being a "loser" with someone whose approval she doesn't need.

If you luck out and your teen is willing to share, patiently listen to her talk about feeling lousy without trying to "fix" her by arguing her feelings. But when she's done, do ask quiet questions to help her start to question herself. Start to build the case that her "I'm a loser" internal voice is a six-year-old bully part of her that likes to keep her down. Perhaps even name it to distinguish it from her other, older and more logical voice: "Is six-year-old 'Suzie' taunting you again? Well, what does sixteen-year-old 'Susan' think about your chances of getting into the play?" and "Whom do you want making decisions about your life: 'Suzie' or 'Susan'? A mean little girl or a smart young woman?" Offer incentives to help your teen overcome her anticipatory fear and feelings of hopelessness: "Well, perhaps you won't get that part, but I'll pay you ten bucks for trying. What do you have to lose?" Then ask her to describe (or maybe write about) her feelings before, during, and after the challenge. The point is to help her see her own distorted thoughts and to then start to trust her more rational ones.

Through it all, be she sharing or not, be sure to remind your teen daily of your love and concern for her. Just as with her old skinned knee, your hugs won't fix her wound, but they sure as heck will lessen the pain.

Self-Injures

"I'm *not* trying to kill myself. I do this to *not* kill myself."

—ELISSA, AGE FIFTEEN

The What

DO

- Stay calm, supportive, and nonjudgmental.
- Expect that your teen will feel very ashamed.
- Ask gently if this was about ending her life. (If so, see "Suicidal, Is," Part 6).
- Know that most self-injury (SI) is *not* about suicide.
- View your teen's SI as a symptom of some other serious pain.
- Understand that she "treats" that pain by hurting herself.
- Tell her that there are better treatments for pain.
- *Ask* if you can see your teen's injuries to determine the need for immediate medical care.
- Be prepared to possibly see extensive damage. (That can be rough.)
- Get your kid to a helper ASAP. (See "Getting Help," Part 9.)

DON'T

- React emotionally.
- Rush her to the hospital unless you suspect suicide.

- *Demand* to see the extent of the hurting if she's too ashamed to show it.
- Blame yourself for not noticing it sooner.
- Be surprised if she says that "all my friends do it." Many do.
- Angrily demand that she stop. (She might just hide it better.)

The Why

SI occurs in various forms, the most common including cutting and burning, where teens (mostly girls) will injure themselves usually in hidden places (upper arms and thighs) typically to superficial extents (although the resultant scarring and infection risks can be serious). As horrendous as self-mutilation can seem, for an increasing number of adolescents it is a "rational" way of handling depression, anxiety, and/or traumatic memories (such as abuse) since this low level of self-hurt is often a protection against total self-destruction. The brain reacts to the induced pain in ways that can alleviate mental anguish. In this view SI can be seen as self-medicating. For other kids who feel emotionally numb (typically from some trauma) the pain they cause themselves often is the only time they report feeling alive. Again, this "crazy" behavior can make a lot of sense to a teen in pain. However, the "medication" of SI not only is physically dangerous but might be addicting as well. Even if you believe that she "only does this to get attention," know that any child willing to mutilate herself to get attention is a person who needs help.

The How

First, read about empathy. (See "Communication/Empathy," Part 9.) Then read it again. Before you confront your child you must get your head in the place where hers is, where the SI behavior actually makes some sense in some way. If you just go crazy with anger, disgust, or hysteria, you'll just push your teen's issues underground, where they can become more deadly. In a weird way, your child's SI is your gift in that it alerts you to serious issues you might have otherwise missed (depression, anxiety, and so on). Once you can signal your empathic understanding to your adolescent, she'll have a much easier time talking about her behavior and seeing that there are much better ways of handling her pain. If she refuses help, gently tell her that you must assume control of this, and insist that she see someone since this is a problem that could hurt her terribly.

WANT TO LEARN MORE?

When Your Child Is Cutting: A Parent's Guide to Helping Children Overcome Self-Injury, by Merry McVey-Noble, et al. (New Harbinger Publications, 2006)

Sleeps Too Little

"A lot of what passes for depression these days is nothing more than a body saying that it needs work."

—GEOFFREY NORMAN

The What

DO

- Monitor for signs of sleep deprivation (irritability, agitation, lethargy, napping, poor focus, poor performance).
- Take this seriously. (Everything in your teenager's life depends on his sleep.)
- Know that he needs ten hours of sleep—that's *per night, not per week.*
- Know that he likely gets six hours on a good night—and insists that's all he needs.

- Know that your teen's brain pushes his sleep demand hours into the night, but he can push it back. (See "Adolescent Brain Development," Part 9.)
- Know that he cannot "stock up for the next week" by sleeping all weekend.
- Look for possible related disorders (depression, anxiety, bipolar disorder, sleep disturbances, drug/alcohol use).
- Get the screens (TV, computer, phone) out of his bedroom. Bribe if you must.
- Get him to try exercising before but not after dinner. (Did I mention bribing?)
- See a physician if this continues because your kid might have unknown sleep disturbances (nightmares, sleep apnea, insomnia, restless leg syndrome).

DON'T

- Allow TV, phones, or computers in bedrooms. (If they're there, bribe them out.)
- Badger, nag, or yell about sleep. (You'll turn a health issue into a wasting war about power and control.)
- Allow long naps (beyond fifteen minutes).
- Use *any* sleeping medications without your physician's approval. (Some can make things worse.)

The Why

Many folks who work with teens consider their lousy sleep habits the number one health issue for today's kids. While it may not sound as dramatic as their high rates of depression, anxiety, suicide, obesity, ADHD, type 2 diabetes, and underachievement, exhaustion plays a powerful role in *each one* of those life-altering threats. Sleep is also a very critical time in an adolescent's day, where most of his growth and development hormones do their thing and where his brain cleans up its neurological clutter. Most research says that your kid needs ten to twelve hours a night. (No, I'm not joking.) I'm ecstatic if my clients get eight hours. Most teens average about six, and that deficit acts like a mismanaged credit card: the constant shortfall just keeps adding to an overdue balance. And no, he can't sleep for sixteen hours on Saturday and Sunday to pay that off. In fact, those marathon sleeps just make everything worse by blowing up the sleep clock in the teen's brain, a structure that needs to set a regular time to zonk out and awaken each day.

A third of our kids stare at their ceilings at midnight because their brains (on their own) advance their sleep clocks a few hours so that they get sleepy at about 1:00 A.M. and awaken at noon. Of course, this means that they're near-comatose during first-period chemistry class. Your kid is not lying when he yells, "I just can't sleep!" What you thought was a desire to party hearty is often adolescent brain rewiring.

The teen's culture makes the bad worse by surrounding him with addicting screens that destroy his brain's "let's sleep now" chemistry in ways that Starbucks would envy. TVs, computers, text screens—these all stimulate and awaken his brain (even though he swears that TV helps him sleep). Add in the unprecedented pressures of contemporary adolescent life and you've got a great recipe for chronic exhaustion. I'm amazed that teens function as well (poorly) as they do. I'm amazed that some can breathe.

The How

Your first step is to see if your kid agrees with any of this (which he likely won't), and then see if he'll agree to work to adjust his sleep clock (which he likely won't). His exhaustion just feels normal to him, and he probably laughs when you say that he needs ten hours of sleep. Many kids see staying up late as a weird rite of passage, bragging about how late they stayed up the night before the exam/game/prom.

So start by asking him to research this topic online on his own and then negotiate (bribe?) for a four-week trial where he gets more sleep and keeps a daily log noting how he feels. Offering incentives is a neat trick since once you get your kid's sleep clock adjusted forward, he'll start to stop staying awake at that new time whether he gets paid or not.

Once your teen is willing, get the screens out of his environment about an hour prior to sleep. This will likely be the toughest part of all for him, so get out your checkbook. Perhaps offer better screens (computer, phone) outside of his room in return for getting rid of the existing ones inside of his room. Or offer extended privileges and freedoms in return for a more responsible sleep schedule (a great bargain). Warn him that his sleep clock will require patient manipulation to reset and that he might get frustrated in the process, but that there are tricks that will eventually get it done. He should play with these until he finds the mix that works. They include:

- Moving bedtime up about fifteen minutes each night (from his usual) until he hits the new target (be sure he doesn't try to go to sleep three hours earlier in one night).
- Getting up at the same time each morning even if he was up late the night before.
- Canning the naps or limiting them to fifteen minutes. (Instead, have him get up and walk/run at nap time.)
- Exercising before (but not after) dinner.
- Turning down his room lights and shutting down all screens one hour prior to bedtime.
- Going decaf from 3:00 P.M. on (chocolate, some sodas, tea, and coffee all have caffeine, which can block the brain's sleep chemicals).

- Reading prior to sleeping.
- Listening to a soothing noise machine and/or relaxation tapes/CDs.
- Trying earplugs.
- Sticking to a nightly sleep ritual, such as showering and snacking at the same time each night.
- Eating sleep-boosting snack foods (pretzels, pasta, turkey).
- Staying calm. Assure him that if he can't sleep well tonight, he'll likely sleep great tomorrow night (if he gets up on time and avoids the nap).

Finally, be sure to put sleep into the same priority basket as appearance and messy rooms, meaning that these are things that aren't worth going to war (where your kid feels that you really hate who he is). Beg and bribe for better sleep, but don't battle. If his sleep becomes a win-lose struggle with parents about who's in charge, insomnia might be in your child's long-term future. Instead try offering incentives for him to handle the downside consequences of not addressing his sleep problem (such as getting up on his own, doing well at school, maintaining his temper, and so on). If he fails to earn what he wants because he's exhausted, he might just decide to get some more shut-eye. Just like with learning, sleep is a thing that you cannot force. In time, most kids figure out that they need sleep to do well in the world. And the less we harass them, the more they'll sleep—eventually.

Smoking Cigarettes, Is

"Of course I can quit. I do it all the time."

—JIMMY, AGE SEVENTEEN

The What

DO

- Know that cigarettes are especially addicting to teen brains, especially the female ones.
- Know that you really can't make your teen stop.
- Know that long-term consequences (disease risks) are not strong deterrents for teens.
- Know that short-term consequences are stronger deterrents (yellow teeth, bad breath, no money, wheezing in gym class).
- Ask/see what smoking does for your teen (calms nerves, feels "cool," gains peer acceptance, provides a way of rebelling?).
- Offer incentives that might provide the same payoffs without the bad breath.
- Offer supports (physician consultation, cessation programs).
- Forbid smoking in your home/car and while driving. (It's a dangerous distraction.)
- Make it clear that smoking will never be OK with you— *because you love her.*

DON'T

- Use health-risk scare tactics. (They can make smoking *more* appealing, especially to the boys.)
- Harass, yell, or punish.
- Buy your teen smokes or give her "dollars for death."
- Conduct "search and destroy" missions for cigs.
- Lose your connection with your kid over cigarettes.

The Why

Here's some contradictory information on smoking. First, know that it's particularly terrible for teens. Beyond the well-known risks of many horrible diseases, teens who smoke seem to become addicted amazingly fast, even with small initial use (particularly girls). Adolescent smoking has also been linked with depression, compromised immune systems, and adult-onset anxiety disorders. So yes, it's terribly bad. And, no, there's not much you can do to stop it—at least in the way you would like to stop it.

Our natural parental reactions to fight this terrible threat turn out to be lousy. Yelling, nagging, and punishing often just increase your kid's urge to smoke. And screaming about her nonfiltered Camels can provoke power and control wars that may lead to more immediate risks: "Mom thinks she won by taking my smokes. Let's see if she can tell that I'm doing pills." And forget putting those pictures of cancer-ridden lungs in her lunch bag. In a Canadian antismoking study the researchers placed the warning sign for poison (that skull and crossbones) on some packages of cigarettes. Guess which became the immediate favorite of teen smokers? Many kids smoke *just* for that "I'm so tough I don't care about dying" image. Others smoke to look cool, to gain peer acceptance, or just because you said that they couldn't. In teen brains, those here-and-now reasons to smoke are not often tamed by consequences that are decades away.

You'll hate me for saying this, but *you really can't stop your teen from smoking* if she's so inclined. And the more that you angrily try to *force* her to stop, the less she'll want to stop, and the better she'll get at hiding her addiction. Parental rage drives the issue underground, where full-blown addiction gets to take over. Know that the only people who quit smoking are those who really, really want to quit. No one else can make this decision for them.

So what can you do? Actually, quite a lot. But you've got to play it smart, not loud.

The How

Focus on here-and-now consequences, but within the limits of your power. Step one is to *ask* if she wants to stop (versus ordering). The odds are that your kid is already conflicted about smoking, so asking respectfully (versus yelling disrespectfully) can empower that smarter part of her that wants to smell better and save money now and wants to live longer in the future. If you hear those joyous words "Yeah, maybe I'd like to stop," then get to your doc ASAP for medical help. Even if your kid says that she'll stop on her own, hearing the physician's wisdom makes it much more possible.

Ask your child what smoking does for her, and then offer incentives that might replace those payoffs. If she digs in and says she's not ready to quit, still offer incentives, but also provide some limiters without making it sound as if she's just being punished for being a bad girl: "Smoking is not OK with me, and it never will be. I know I can't stop you, but I will do everything I can to encourage you to stop. So you cannot smoke in our home, car, or presence, and I must escrow your allowance since I won't finance suicide."

One final shot you can take at a dug-in teen smoker is to appeal to her exploding adolescent needs for power and control. Frame smoking as a loss of personal freedom to some coldhearted bastards: "Honey, I have a hard time seeing how you're OK with being controlled by addictive chemicals marketed by pushers who profit from disease and death."

Then, as hard as it may be, put the smoking issue aside (except for keeping the quitting incentives always on the table) and work on the positives of your relationship and stay close to your kid's heart. Hang out with her as much as possible *especially* while she's still fighting the cigs. If you can be this disciplined and help her make her own decision to quit, she'll likely avoid dog breath for the rest of her life.

WANT TO LEARN MORE?

Buttheads: Teens Write About the Perils of Smoking, by Youth Communication (Youth Communication, 2005)

Smoking 101: An Overview for Teens (Teen Overviews), Library Binding, by Margaret O. Hyde and John F. Setaro (Twenty-First Century Books, 2005)

Stressed, Is

"WHAT? WE'RE OUT OF TWINKIES? AAARRRRGGGHHH!!!"

—AUTHOR'S UNNAMED CHILD

The What

DO

- Know that this is the most stressed generation of teens we've ever seen.
- Know that high stress zaps the brain chemicals your teen needs to cope with his world.
- Listen quietly if he yells nonabusively. Look for themes (clues) in his ranting. (See "Communication/Empathy," Part 9.)
- Model calmness in the face of your teen's craziness. (Calm is contagious.)
- Watch for indicators of chronic high stress (shifts in sleeping/eating patterns, fretting, risky behaviors, crying, frequent outbursts of anger).
- Try to help your teen improve his diet, sleep, and exercise. (These can make *huge* differences.)

- Evaluate your child's schedule, and cut back on demands, at least temporarily.
- Ask if he wishes that he wasn't alive. (See "Suicidal, Is," Part 6.)
- See a helper if your teen's high stress continues for more than a week. (See "Getting Help," Part 9.)

DON'T

- Underestimate the risks of excessive stress.
- Increase your kid's stress by yelling back or mocking him.
- Give him hollow reassurances. ("You'll be fine.")
- Discount his pain. ("Oh, honey, everybody's stressed these days.")
- Take charge and make decisions for him unless he's in really bad shape.

The Why

In the proper dose, stress is actually a healthy part of an adolescent's development. But in overdose, it can cripple and even kill. Today's teens are pounded with overt and covert stressors more than any other generation we've measured. The obvious stresses come from increasingly demanding academics, college entrance competition, and athletics (many high school sports now "unofficially" demand year-round commitments). The hidden stresses come from a culture that confronts your child with terribly complex sex/drugs/violence decisions at insanely young ages when he has neither the neurology nor the life experience to help him navigate. (See "Adolescent Brain Development" and "Adolescent Culture" in Part 9.)

Stress overdose is often overlooked by parents since the ability of teens to tolerate stress can vary a lot. (What was fun for your daughter might be agonizing for your son.) And the biochemical effects of excessive stress on the brain can lead kids to do screwy, high-risk things to feel better. (Risk activities create surges in stress-depleted neurotransmitters.) This is how that "perfect" kid suddenly finds himself with his pedal to the metal, doing what he knows is crazy and wrong and feeling terrific for about ten minutes. Those biochemical effects can also cause his brain to wish that it were no longer alive.

The How

If your teen goes crazy over missing Twinkies, don't go crazy in response. He's making no sense because he's really screaming about other things that hurt a lot more than Twinkie withdrawal. Love him enough to listen to his rant to see where it goes. (As he keeps yelling, that lost Twinkie may suddenly morph into his lost girlfriend, his lost ability to do chemistry, and five other losses you knew nothing about.) View these rants as gifts, as pressure-relief valves that keep him from blowing apart, and as ways that can help you learn more about his stressors.

If he just suffers in silence, approach your teen with your concerns, but don't insist (badger/nag) that he talk: "I'm worried that you're under a lot of stress. I'd love it if we could talk about that, or perhaps you'd rather chat with a counselor. Please let me know. You don't have to feel so bad." Teens often have self-imposed rules against admitting to being stressed (it's "weak") and often try to do the impossible without complaining. Sometimes unexpressed stress can overwhelm a kid to the point where he'd rather not be alive. Never hesitate to ask him straight out about that.

Try to help your child see that (1) he is stressed out and (2) there are things that can help. Exercise might be the first thing to suggest (it often leads to better sleep and appetite), but it's the last thing kids think they need. At least thirty minutes a day of cardio work can equal the good effects of many medications and improve only about a million other things in a kid's life. (See your doc for approval and a plan.) Brisk walks work great. Treadmills become tolerable to teens when they're attached to screens (TV). Punching bags are terrific stress relievers, cardio workers, and aggression antidotes. As are tai chi, meditation, yoga, karate—the list is endless, but your kid's time is not, so try things that might actually fit into his (and your) schedule. This is why in-home activities work best over time.

Junk foods cause junk moods and worsen stress. If you're unfamiliar with nutrition, go see an expert together to design a better diet. Your teen will also need ten hours of sleep each night to handle his twenty-six-hour days (stop laughing—OK, settle for eight). (See "Sleeps Too Little," Part 3.)

In all of these discussions, do as little of the decision making as possible. The more your kid takes charge of this, the less his efforts will fizzle out after a week, since they'll be his efforts, not yours.

WANT TO LEARN MORE?

Fighting Invisible Tigers: A Stress Management Guide for Teens, by Earl Hipp (Free Spirit Publishing, 2008)

Hot Stones and Funny Bones: Teens Helping Teens Cope with Stress and Anger, by Brian Seaward (HCI Teens, 2002)

PART 4

HOME ISSUES

Umm... How about we have band practice at your house instead?

AH, YES. HOME sweet home. That warm, wonderful place where teens often feel so secure, so special, and so loved that they return the favor by acting so nasty. Uncle Harry wouldn't even believe you if you told him. "A pigsty for a room?" he'd ask skeptically. "At my house she was as neat as a pin. And you say that she's rude? That's really hard to believe. She was all about 'please' and 'thank you' with us. She's quite the perfect little lady as far as we're concerned. Perhaps you're being a little tough on her?"

Before you unclench your teeth to shriek at Uncle Harry, know that many teenagers have a befuddling policy of acting the worst with those who love them the best, namely their parents. Nowhere does familiarity breed more contempt than around the hearth of a home with teenagers. It's really quite amazing. Wonderful teen things like polished manners, positive attitudes, and helpfulness—these often seem to get stored in the garage to be picked up when leaving the house, only to be dropped off on the way back in. The kid who eats at home as if she'd been raised by wolves morphs into Deborah Kerr at Uncle Harry's house, softly sipping soup as if she's at the Plaza Hotel.

This phenomenon has to do with struggles of parenting and "teenagering," where issues of power and control often blow up any peace in the home. (See "Identity," "Adolescent Psychological Development," and "Parenting Teenagers," Part 9.) Snorting (versus sipping) soup is a choice made politically. Since Uncle Harry is not in control of her life, your teen can show off the great manners you've taught her, the same ones she'll never show you at home because, well, *you demand that she does.* And right now she's busy proving that she's so totally different and independent from you. That's just nature's way.

So don't take this stuff personally, and don't assume that what you see at home is the behavior you get when your teenager is out in the world. As her beloved parents, you'll get the worst of your teen's behaviors for a while, until your child matures a bit.

And if it helps you stay calm in the face of temporary outrageousness, silently remember nature's greatest payback; in not too many years, she'll have children of her own, and then. . . .

Adoption, Has Issues With

"Mom, we did a family genetics project today, and something weird came up . . . is there something you want to tell me?"

The What

DO

- Proudly and publicly affirm that your child is adopted from day one.

- Let him speak without interruption, no matter how hard that is. ("Mom, you always loved my brother more.")
- Affirm his feelings, no matter how painful they are. ("I can see how you could feel less loved by me.")
- Allow/encourage contact with the biological family, no matter how threatening that feels (as long as they are safe).
- Help your child feel that you love him so much that he can say tough things to you.
- Reassure him only after he's done speaking.

DON'T

- Hide the fact or avoid talking about the adoption.
- Interrupt to make him feel better. ("Honey, of course we love you the same.")
- Discount your teen's feelings. ("Oh, sweetheart, you don't really feel like that.")
- Let your own fears of losing your kid dictate your responses. ("How could you say that you want to be with your biological mom after all we've done for you?")

The Why

Adoption is a very tricky concept for chosen kids (a great label to use). Adoptive parents often forget this since in their head the adopted child feels as much theirs as do their biological ones. For the parents, that uncertain adjustment phase is usually a onetime, early-on event. But chosen kids keep revisiting this issue throughout their lives in different ways as they grow and understand more, often feeling different, less loved, and abandoned even in the most loving of homes. When this nagging uncertainty collides with the issues of adolescence, all hell can break loose. Chosen teens often set off in searches (physical and emotional) for their unknown biological parents or start to speak of moving in with the ones they know. The fact of their adoption can become a convenient dumping ground upon which to vent all of the normal strife of adolescence. What you want to avoid is having the biological family become perceived as the magical antidote to all of the child's pain. If left in the fantasy stage, that reunification dream can become a growth-crippling obsession, leading the child away from many critical things such as conflict resolution skills and continued bonding with his adoptive family.

The How

The best antidote for dangerous fantasy is calm reality. Here that means to normalize the adoption concept as much as possible. The term should be used freely and comfortably within a family so that the child sees this as a shame-free event, one to be celebrated, not hidden away. (Some families commemorate "adoption day" in addition to birthday.)

Allow your teen to speak as much as possible about all of his adoption feelings, *especially* the scary ones like wanting to be with his adoptive family. (See "Communication/Empathy," Part 9.) Do not resist his urges to see his biological family. In fact, welcome those things as the normal and healthy wishes that they are. Try not to see this as losing your child but rather as a way to strengthen your relationship. When you set aside your own needs to honor his, he will see you as loving him to an extent that no other relationship could ever match. And as his fantasy-based dreams diminish with real-life contact, his reality-based love for you will grow.

Bedroom, Has a Pigsty For

"Honey, I can live with the mess—I just get freaked when it starts to move around."

—MILLIE, AGE FORTY-NINE

The What

DO

- Calmly ask for some effort, telling her that *you* are a tad neurotic.
- Offer some incentive for relative (not perfect) neatness.
- Offer to work with her once a week to shovel things out.
- Tolerate messiness, but only in your teen's own room.
- Thank your kid profusely whenever you catch her being neat. Say that it helps you feel better.

DON'T

- Nag or yell.
- Make fun of your child's room to others.
- Allow her messiness to spread to common areas.
- Maintain her room for her. (Unless you are hiring her a lifetime maid service.)
- Go to war, where she feels that you *really, personally* dislike who she is because she's messy.

The Why

Messy (meaning most) teens don't understand adult demands for neatness. They often see it as senseless control and power needs on our part, as a great exercise for wasting time. The more we push, the more they dig in as part of their healthy need to push away from adults a bit and find their own way on things. This is actually a critical part of their identity building. (See "Identity," Part 9.) Most teen brains are not yet wired to need neatness. That habit occurs later in life *and has nothing to do with the heart (character) of your kid.* Beg, borrow, or bribe (use incentives) as well as you can, but this is definitely a second-priority concern.

The How

Remember how fast the past few years flew by? The next few will race a lot faster. When you're waving good-bye to your kid as she goes off to college or the military, how important will her messiness seem then? And how will you feel then about what you are about to say to her now? Use that picture to calm your neurotic nerves, and then give her a messy hug. By the way, how neat were you as a teen? If your answer is "very," ask yourself, "Why?"

Computer, Uses Excessively

"MySpace: Where men are men, women are women, and kids are predators or cops."

—ANONYMOUS INTERNET QUOTE

The What

DO

- Know that your kid's computer is your old "corner" (place to hang out with friends).
- Understand that some bad *but more good* happens on the electronic "corner."
- Keep his computer in public or semipublic areas (not the bedroom).
- Allow computer privacy in relation to your teen's level of responsibility.
- Look to see if his other interests (sleep, grades, sports, work) are suffering.
- Ask him to set a reasonable daily limit, and then review his logged hours after a week.

- Look to see how much time is spent on which activity (games, chats, homework, surfing).
- If (or when) your teen's use wildly exceeds his goal, ask him what he can do to cut back his use.
- Repeat this for a few weeks, asking him to take charge of the issue.
- Offer rewards for reduced use. (See "Bribes/Incentives," Part 9.)
- Gently raise the point that computer use may be addicting for some folks.
- If he can't get control, get him to a helper. (See "Getting Help," Part 9.)
- Pull the plug, but *only as a last resort*, and immediately set up a plan to get him back online but under your time control until he can self-regulate.

DON'T

- Immediately pull that plug (unless you enjoy explosions).
- Underestimate how important that screen can be to your kid.
- Assume that all computer time is bad for your teen.
- Look to eliminate all computer use. (He'll miss out on a lot of good.)
- Give up and approve of his staying up all night at a keyboard.
- Allow totally unsupervised access.

The Why

Like it or not, the Internet has largely replaced the old soda shop as *the* afterschool source of teen socialization, a function that is critical to adolescent development. While many contemporary parents wistfully long for the old soda shop, their own parents might have opted for the Web since bad teen things happened out in the old "real" world as least as much as they do online. And the research surprisingly suggests that those online interactions can help with teen development just as the soda shop used to. But there can also be a downside, which is likely why you're reading this. Screens can be addictive and can start to stop your teen's other activities. (Did you ever hang out too much as a teen?) Balanced use is fine, but when he starts to live exclusively through a keyboard, it's time to intervene.

The How

Start softly with the least intrusive measures and slowly turn up the control, but only as you need. The idea is for your teenager to *learn for himself* how to self-regulate. If you just yank the plug (and live to tell the tale), the tale you'll tell is how he learned how to be offline only when you were around (and then went screen insane in college). Keep in mind that the idea of your kid having zero computer use would be about the equivalent of a permanent grounding to your adolescent self. The key, as with most everything adolescent, is for him to achieve a workable balance that becomes his own idea, one that he'll keep for a lifetime and that will serve as a model for him to use with other, future addicting behaviors.

WANT TO LEARN MORE?

Teens and Computers . . . What's a Parent to Do? A Basic Guide to Social Networking, Instant Messaging, Chat, Email, Computer Set-up and More, by Donna S. Bast (BookSurge Publishing, 2007)

Driving, Starts

"Never lend your car to anyone to whom you have given birth."

—ERMA BOMBECK

The What

DO

- Know that researchers have MRIs suggesting that a sixteen-year-old brain isn't ready to drive. (See "Adolescent Brain Development," Part 9.)
- Know that Hertz (the car rental company) has statistics suggesting that a twenty-four-year-old brain *still* isn't ready to drive well.
- Make your own assessment of your teen's brain (via her behaviors and not just her age) before handing over a key.
- Insist on driver's ed, good emotional control, and decent grades as key "key" prerequisites.
- Allow no more than one passenger and no unsupervised night driving for at *least* one year, and no phone use while driving *ever*. (These are high teen crash factors.)
- Write out and sign a "No Drug Use for Car Use" agreement. (Note that alcohol is a drug.)
- Make contributions to car maintenance and insurance part of the deal.

DON'T

- Hand three thousand pounds of 100 mph metal to a sixteen-year-old without lots of thought and preparation.
- Underestimate how important driving might be to your kid. (You can use this as a growth incentive.)
- Be surprised if your teen *declines* getting her license. Record numbers of teens now see driving as too difficult for sixteen-year-olds. (Those might be the only teens we should allow to drive.)

The Why

Unrestricted driving at age sixteen has long been a sacred adolescent entitlement, an altar at which we've sacrificed too many lives
for too long. A sixteen-year-old driver is *twenty times* more likely
than her parent to die behind the wheel and *three times* more
likely than even her eighteen-year-old brother. Many experts are
finally asserting the insanity of this teen-driver notion in the light
of our newer understanding of adolescent brains. Driving is one
of those adult functions that you perform so often that many
forget how complex it really is. Many sixteen-year-olds simply
don't have the wiring needed to *even begin to properly learn*
this intricate and potentially lethal task, let alone do it well. The
same folks who would never allow a sixteen-year-old to carry a
concealed handgun seem to have no problem giving her control
of a potentially deadlier weapon. Yet the fact remains that teen
driving has a huge upside in allowing employment, activities,
and family help (driving her bratty brother to soccer)—things
that she'd miss out on without a license. So, dear parent, here's
another one of those exquisite parenting dilemmas for multiple
sleepless nights. You were sleeping too much anyway, right?

The How

If you're ready to let your child drive, do so only with lots of safety
precautions as noted earlier, and only after deciding whether your
particular kid is ready for this, regardless of her age. The critical
judgments you must make concern your kid's emotional control
and level of maturity. Impulsiveness, explosiveness, aggression,
peer-influence susceptibility, risk taking, poor judgment capabilities, drug and alcohol use—these are all common teen issues, and
each one signals potential highway tragedy. If your child presents
any of these "symptoms," set up a plan where she earns steps
toward driving (driver's ed, getting her permit, practice driving

sessions with you) by demonstrating growth in controlling those symptoms. ("Honey, if you can go a month without losing your temper, you're ready to sign up for that driver's ed course.") And before you even think about teaching your own kid to drive, consider first having your own "expert" driving skills evaluated by a real expert. You will likely be astounded (as I was) to see how lousy even we adult drivers are at that game. By the way, my expert said that the last person on the planet he would instruct would be his own child. He says they already have enough to fight about.

WANT TO LEARN MORE?

Crashproof Your Kids: Make Your Teen a Safer, Smarter Driver, by Timothy C. Smith (Fireside, 2006)

Hates His Parents

"I'll never speak to you again . . . and this time I'm *not* changing my mind!"

—SARAH, AUTHOR'S DAUGHTER, AGE FIVE

The What

DO

- Know that to teens hate usually means to be annoyed at with or frustrated with.
- Know that it is normal (and OK) for younger teens to occasionally "hate" their parents.
- Know that it's not normal (or OK) for any teen to hate his parents most of the time.
- Ask your teen to join with you to get some help for the *family, not just for him.*

- Accept your kid's "hate" statements without argument. He likely loves you, and that's why he "hates" you—he's trying to work something out, and you're in the way.
- Tell your teen you're sorry you make him so angry and you do love him even though he "hates" you.
- Ask what you can do to help.
- Welcome your teen's words, even the angry ones. If he's talking to you at all, that's a start!
- See a helper if your kid's winter doesn't thaw to spring within a few weeks. (See "Getting Help," Part 9.)

DON'T

- Assume it's normal for a teen to hate you most of the time.
- Take this stuff personally. You are the stage on which your child will act out his conflicts.
- Hate the word *hate*. Listen for what's behind that hateful word.

The Why

As parents we have a strange double standard for speech. Often we curse all the time yet go crazy if our child copies us. (See "Curses," Part 2.) Similarly we'll "hate" the Dallas Cowboys (the football team) as they beat up our team, and then at halftime we'll go off on our kid for saying that he "hates" us for something such as not allowing that coed sleepover (which you will never allow, right?). The fact is that his telling you that he hates you is a thing called *communication*, a tool that can open the door to problem solving and eventual closeness if we're tough enough to play it smart. Because, as with marriages, it's the cold silence that is more worrisome. So view you teen's "hate speech" as his request to talk.

The How

Sidestep your teen's provocative words. (This is about frustration, not genocide.) Acknowledge his anger, and ask him to tell you why he's angry. (See "Communication/Empathy," Part 9.) If repeated chats get everyone nowhere but angrier, it's time to see a helper. (See "Getting Help," Part 9.) Do not accept protracted anger as being normal for teens, but view it as a smoke alarm telling you there's trouble in the home and now is the time to find it before it grows.

WANT TO LEARN MORE?

Staying Connected to Your Teenager: How to Keep Them Talking to You and How to Hear What They're Really Saying, by Michael Riera (Perseus Publishing, 2003)

Home Alone, Is Left

"If you must choose between leaving your sixteen-year-old or your six-year-old home alone, consider leaving the six-year-old. He might be safer."

The What

DO

- Know that almost all teen risk behaviors occur when grownups are not nearby.
- Know that adolescents are not small adults—they are *large children.*
- Know that teens often get sad and scared when left alone too much (though they'll rarely admit this).

- Know that while they want you out of their sight, they usually want you in their house (they'll never admit that).
- Know that while their intentions may be perfect, their frontal lobes are not. (See "Adolescent Brain Development," Part 9.)
- Understand that at the touch of one button two hundred equally challenged teens can instantly know that your kid is home alone. (Can you text P-A-R-T-Y?)
- Provide adult supervision for lengthy parent absences.
- Push adult-supervised activities that keep your teen busy in the afternoon if no one is home after school.
- Insist on knowing your teen's whereabouts as a condition of her going out. (Teens usually know whose house is empty and when.)

DON'T

- Assume that your kid is as mature cognitively as she looks physically.
- Put her into a situation for which she's not prepared (such as two hundred teenagers at the front door).
- Invade your teen's personal space; just provide a subtle safety fence around it.

The Why

Many experts say that, left home alone, young children are less at risk than are teenagers. (Of course, leaving either is a bad idea.) They know that one of Mother Nature's best jokes is installing child brains into adult bodies (teenagers) that are designed to push limits. Adolescents are creatures still in need of parenting—caretaking of a different sort for sure, but nonetheless parenting, which includes a system that puts limits on options for risky behavior. (See "Parenting Teenagers," Part 9.) Responsible adults within earshot are terrific limiters of risky behaviors. And if you have that outstanding teen who's incredibly mature and reliable, know that the adult "veneer" on those perfect kids can be about two microns thick. Change a few variables and the wheels can come off that wagon in about the time it takes a neighbor to call 911. Is that an unfair judgment of your responsible child? Very possibly. But how exactly would you care to find out?

The How

Home-alone weekends for adolescents are just a very bad idea. If you doubt that, you must not be reading your local police reports. (In just a few years she'll be off to college, and then you can go away for as many weekends as you like.) Even those three afternoon hours every weekday pose a great teen risk for working parents (which includes most of us). Much bad goes down from 3:00 to 6:00 P.M. since those alone times are so predictable. Adolescent brains may have judgment issues, but they can tell time very well. Working parents should provide activities, "teen sitters," or at least random afternoon visits from Grandma to disrupt the potential for planning for the bad. Unpredictable phone check-in calls on land lines (versus mobile cell phones) are helpful as well: "Hi, honey. Just checking in to see how your biology presentation went. I've always been fascinated by the mating rituals of wildebeests."

Do this smoothly enough, and your teen will never know which wildebeests you were actually worried about.

Privacy, Demands

"The right to be let alone is indeed the beginning of all freedom."

—WILLIAM O. DOUGLAS

The What

DO

- Understand that your teen's privacy likely means more to him than yours does to you.
- Know that the more you respect his privacy, the less he will keep from you.
- Know that the more you invade his privacy, the more tempting risky behaviors can become.
- Know that having a private retreat space (his room) is a good remedy for bad moods.
- Tell your kid that he's the one who will decide how much privacy he deserves according to his behavior.
- Increase/decrease his rights of privacy according to his increasing/decreasing levels of responsibility.
- Extend privacy to your teen's room, diaries, phone, e-mail, and personal conversations if he's doing OK.
- Tell him up front that you will always check on any Web postings. These are "highway billboards" anyone can see, and they can pose safety concerns.

DON'T

- Invade your teen's privacy without "reasonable cause." That can create problems that would not have otherwise existed.
- Extend privacy rights to Net pages.
- Say that you have an unconditional right to invade your teenager's life without cause. That's how insurrections begin.
- Permit total privacy if your child is engaged in high-risk behaviors (such as drugs or sex).

The Why

The disquieting fact is that for your kid to grow up well he must have some degree of privacy in which to explore his identity and say and do things he wouldn't if he knew you were watching. (See "Identity," Part 9.) E-mails, text messages, phone conversations, and letters (yes, these antiques are occasionally still used) are all places where a responsible kid should be given the benefit of the (privacy) doubt. All Web pages, blogs, and so on must be monitored by you since these can present predation risks with the extensive personal information kids post. The trick is in the balancing of privacy with safety. But that formula is not as straightforward as you might think.

If you are a fan of TV shrinks and love their "I own your room, and I'll search whenever I like" policies, know that those can cost you dearly since they delay your child's development into a trustworthy human and encourage "jailbreak" insanity once he's away from you (such as at college). Overpolicing your child also sends the message that he is not trustworthy, and that can breed anger and resentment that can push him in the direction of the unsafe behaviors. ("Since they assume that I do sex and drugs, I might as well do them.") Underpolicing sends the message that you don't really care, and anything goes. The gold is in that middle position, where you always are eager to give your child privacy and you make it clear that he is in charge of this issue: "Son, I hate being a spy. As long as you're doing well, I will not invade your space. That will change if you make dangerous behavior decisions." You want him learning to self-regulate while he's still under your roof, but you also want him surviving long enough to leave. (See "Parenting Teenagers," Part 9.)

The How

The cops have a good set of privacy rules you might want to adopt. They invade your space only when they have "probable cause," meaning very clear evidence that you are into something bad. Just wondering if you are into something bad is not sufficient for cops, and it shouldn't be for parents. Just what constitutes parental probable cause is up to you, but that list might include repeated drug or sex infractions, patterns of significant behavior changes (grades, friends, moods), or suicidal indicators. (See "Suicidal, Is," Part 6.) If you must roll back your teenager's privacy, be sure to also set up the target behaviors with which he can earn back your trust and respect. And yes, privacy is trust and respect, which is why it must be handled so carefully. Just routinely searching your child's things as a way of parenting your kid is likely to have the same result as if your local police tossed your home periodically whenever they felt like it. Yes, that might deter some illegal behavior, but the anger and resentment it would inspire would outweigh any potential gains by far. That is how revolutions begin. Remember, your best weapon against the insanity around your child is your *relationship* with him. Think long and hard before you gamble that away for a room search that likely will turn up nothing but a lot of bad feelings.

WANT TO LEARN MORE?

Staying Connected to Your Teenager: How to Keep Them Talking to You and How to Hear What They're Really Saying, by Michael Riera (Perseus Publishing, 2003)

Yes, Your Teen Is Crazy! Loving Your Kid Without Losing Your Mind, by Michael J. Bradley (Harbor Press, 2003)

Religion, Rejects Parents'

"A religious awakening which does not awaken the sleeper to love has roused him in vain."

—JESSAMYN WEST

The What

DO

- Stay calm. If your religion is important to you, know that you are about to shape its future with your child, for better or for worse.
- Know that adolescents are just beginning to understand what spirituality is about.
- Congratulate yourself. Your teen's testing skepticism is your proof of *successful*, not failed, parenting.
- Know that most people become less religious in adolescence and early adulthood.
- Know that most of those who come back to the faith of their parents do so if their teenage religious views are tolerated with love and respect.
- Ask from where your teen's "code" originates (right and wrong, ethics of behavior, significance of life) since she has rejected yours.
- Allow exploration of other religions. (Encourage her to find a spiritual identity; see "Identity," Part 9.)

DON'T

- Attempt to angrily compel a love of your religion. (Adolescent spirituality must be embraced freely, never forced.)

- Hide your spiritual values from your child. (She'll watch you to decide how relevant they are.)
- Worry that your teen's exposure to other religions will negate your own.

The Why

Research shows teenagers are more religious/spiritual than most parents would guess and finds that religious kids tend to be among the safest and happiest teens in the culture. It also reveals that (as with most things) parents hold the greatest influence over the religious futures of their children, *both pro and con*, and that's where the excruciating dilemma lies when a child rises up to challenge or reject their faith. Loving parents who patiently tolerate their teens' disparate religious views are the ones who most often get to welcome them back one day as adults sharing the same beliefs. Those who go to war with their children over faith have little chance of seeing them in the congregation—ever.

The How

Your kid's initial presentation of spiritual searching might initially appear as an insulting dodge to get to sleep late, and while it might be just that, you can turn this into something much more important. The wise parent sidesteps this provocation and instead returns it as a quiet challenge to the child: "Well, if you're old enough to reject my religion, then you're old enough to tell me about your own. When I get back from services, I'll ask that we go out for a coffee because I need to know where your life code originates. You do have a code to live by, right? See you in two." The idea is to get those wheels turning inside that adolescent brain on these critical identity issues: "Geeezzz, I never thought she'd ask me that. What the heck *do* I believe? Where *do* good and bad come from?" Offer incentives if your teen is on the fence about attending, but remember that your primary goal is to help her develop her spiritual identity, not become an extension of your own. As much as you may want to demand your teen's participation, keep in mind that having a family war over religion can teach your child to forever hate the thing you love. If you can show her the strength of tolerance and the patience of love in the face of her rejecting something sacred to you, then she might begin to wonder where you got that kind of power. And that might be the best sales pitch you could ever make for your beliefs.

When it comes to teenagers and religion, remember that old adage about setting people free to see if you truly have their hearts. Ask yourself what the good might be in forcing a body into worshiping if the heart is elsewhere, angry.

WANT TO LEARN MORE?

Soul Searching: The Religious and Spiritual Lives of American Teenagers, by Christian Smith and Melinda Lundquist Denton (Oxford University Press, 2005)

Rules, Refuses

"I didn't miss curfew—Dude, it's only 8:00 P.M. in Rangoon."

The What

DO

- Speak more of *expectations*, less of *rules.*
- Always state the motivation behind the rule (because you, like, *love* him).
- See repeatedly disregarded rules as symptoms of problems, not insults or challenges.

- Know that the rule least observed is the one unilaterally imposed.
- Know that the rule most observed is the one mutually negotiated.
- Know that fewer rules = more adherence.
- Know that clear and simple rules = more compliance.
- Tell your teen five things he's doing right for every one thing he's doing wrong.
- Keep rules as a *minor* part of your relationship.
- Use *consequences*, not *punishments*, for infractions. (See "Parenting Teenagers," Part 9.)
- Get help ASAP if the broken rules are life threatening and/or if the refusals continue. (See "Getting Help," Part 9.)

DON'T

- Go nuts over rule violations. Stay cool to figure out the *illness* behind that *symptom*.
- Have a zillion rules. (West Point is for volunteers—your kid got drafted.)
- Have zero expectations. (That feels like zero caring.)
- Let rules become the focus of your relationship with your kid. (When rules rule the relationship, the relationship is toast.)
- Criticize any more than you absolutely must.

The Why

When families and teens see shrinks about "rules fights," the shrinks often make everyone mad by not talking about the *rules* and instead talking about the *relationships*. The research shows that having many rules without a relationship works badly and having a relationship with few rules works great. Effective relationships work out the rules stuff with hardly anyone noticing. Close parent/teen connections mean that the family is in the habit

of calmly sharing views about things like curfew and easily negotiating agreements that both sides can accept. These families have
to think twice when you ask them what their "rules" are. They
sort of make it up as they go along, which, by the way, is another
indicator of family success since "rules" with teens must be constantly adjusted according to their age and level of responsibility.
So be flexible. If the family doesn't learn how to bend, it will
break.

The How

Always be clear about your *expectations* for your child, but avoid
conveying these as chapter-and-verse rules as much as possible.
Expectations can sound like loving concerns; *rules* can sound like
stupid speed limits. Starting in the delivery room, you should be
letting your child know that you expect him to be responsible,
safe, and respectful (AKA no drugs, sex, or violence). But you
want to have these things seen by your teen more as *values to be
embraced* and less as senseless restrictions to be fought. If you
have constant fights over rules, go back to the values sharing
first to explain *why* those things are important to you—which is
really because *you want his life to be good*. As silly as it sounds,
most families forget that critical fact as they get consumed by the
anger and control fights of the rules wars. *It's really about parental love*. Conversely, no expectations or limits = no love.

Repeat that about ten thousand times to remind yourself and
him exactly why you are making his life miserable. Then negotiate (or offer to renegotiate) the rules as expressions of those
values that are expressions of your love: "I can't go for the later
curfew for a while because of your drinking episodes. I love you
too much to risk your getting hurt. But your friends are welcome
here anytime." *Negotiate* does not mean "cave in." You are still
the CEO of your family corporation, and you make the final call.

But in making that call you entertain all comments, suggestions, and requests that your kid offers, and you compromise wherever possible (AKA whenever it's not life-threatening—see "Decision Making," Part 9). Be sure that even if the two of you disagree vehemently about the "rule," you both leave that disagreement very clear about the reason for the rule—a thing called the love of a parent for a child.

WANT TO LEARN MORE?

Uncommon Sense for Parents with Teenagers, by Michael Riera (Celestial Arts, 2004)

Yes, Your Teen Is Crazy! Loving Your Kid Without Losing Your Mind, by Michael J. Bradley (Harbor Press, 2003)

PART 5

SCHOOL ISSUES

NOTE: BEFORE PROCEEDING, you must write the following bumper sticker slogan a hundred times. This is mandatory. Spelling counts. *"They can force me to go to school, but they can't make me learn anything."*

Just kidding—you don't have to write anything. But wasn't that annoying, being told what to learn and how to learn it? Didn't you have an immediate urge to resist that order? Imagine how our kids feel. That's pretty much what their lives are like twenty-four/seven.

It's weird how we ex-kids (parents) forget how difficult school can be. Not only do we repress those painful memories (such as how agonizingly slowly a clock can tick), but we also start to build this weird fantasy about how enjoyable school should be for our children. It's often not enjoyable for our children, and as teens they begin to react just like you did a moment ago—they get annoyed and oppositional, and they don't do what they're told. That's when we have one of those painful parent realizations that we can't control our teens the way we'd wish. These insights wash over us like large waves of astonishment and frustration. And among these waves sometimes comes a tsunami regarding school performance.

That bumper sticker perfectly summarizes the dilemma of parents concerning their school-challenged children. Forcing a kid to learn is like forcing him to sleep: the more you angrily fight about it, the less he'll sleep—or learn. Using force to reach goals like these doesn't work very well. In fact, economists call that a "diminishing return" strategy, meaning the more you do, the less you get.

So should you helplessly throw up your hands after getting those infuriating notes from your teen's teachers? (My favorite was the one that seemed to imply that I "allow" my kid to screw up at school: "Dear Parent: I am very concerned that your son somehow feels it's OK to come unprepared to class. . . .") In fact there are many things that we can do to help our academically ailing adolescents. But as that serenity prayer suggests, first decide on what you can do and forget about what you can't.

In the education struggles, that means conceding certain things from the get-go, such as the fact that school is often boring and irrelevant—to most kids. It's also indisputably the best path to a good life, although teens often find it hard to worry about what might happen a decade from now. So I tell my school-challenged teen clients that school is not boring and irrelevant but is actually irrelevant and boring. This fact has actually been studied. (If you doubt this, answer quick: what was the gross national product of Yugoslavia in 1973, when you were forced to memorize stuff you cared nothing about?) If you insist on not conceding this, then please explain how you force someone to experience rapture in resolving quadratic equations. "Learning for the joy of learning" is an adult experience that most kids just don't get and may not get for several years. There are the exceptions, but they're pretty rare. Students are mostly draftees, not volunteers.

A metaphor that works well for school-struggling teens is to say that school is like baseball: you play hard in the minors to one day drive a red Corvette. A great average in a lower minor league (middle school) gets you into a better minor league (high school college prep), which gets you into the major leagues (skill training or college), which gets you the keys to that convertible. Kids can accept the "illogic" of school if you say that it's a game to get you into the next game. In that light, don't hesitate to offer incentives for good grades. (See "Bribes/Incentives," Part 9.) While these sound like a mercenary contamination of something that many hold sacred (education), these tricks can kick-start your resistant learner to take a shot. As he experiences success, that "joy of learning" and achievement stuff can begin to grow within him. (See "Parenting Teenagers," Part 9.)

And while you're conceding things, immediately hand over the real power here to your kid. Whether she's under- or over-achieving, you must start from the premise that she and she alone will ultimately decide whether any changes will occur. That's just the sad fact. But the hope-filled fact is that there are lots of things you can do to *help* her make a decision to change. These you'll find listed in this section, all embracing a common wisdom about dealing with tsunamis.

After floods hit, we must work with what Mother Nature presents to us, building dikes, jetties, and flood channels and elevating homes to minimize the damage from a thing we can't control. We even have ways of using nature's own momentum against her, to redirect her power to build shorelines rather than to wipe them out. It does little to simply rage at the waters except to make us feel temporarily better and then permanently hopeless.

It's much the same with our school-challenged children. We must accept them for who they are in relation to school and then tweak that as well as we can while we await the intellectual awakening and study discipline that almost always eventually blossoms—*if we're wise enough not to go toe-to-toe in bitter, judgmental, and demoralizing rages with our kids.* Our anger only delays or kills off that wondrous maturation, and it can bring on terrible new problems of behavior that can make the old problems of achievement look like stupid things over which to have started a war.

Mother Nature also provides safety nets for school-challenged adolescents. She gives us earth on which to build community colleges. I once received a letter from a chronic high school underachiever with whom I worked. It read, "Hey, Doc Mike! Guess where I'm graduating from next week—no, it's not Edison [our local juvenile prison]. It's NYU! HA! You'd never have guessed that I could do that, right? Tell the truth. . . ." Michele went on to describe how she went to a community college, learned the discipline of study, and then parlayed that into a degree from a fine university.

I was never able to "cure" Michele. But I was able to help her parents shift their approach from the anger and rejection of punishment to the support and acceptance of love. It was very hard for them, for they believed as most of us do that it is an act of love to rage at a school-challenged child. It is not. They never saw Michele on an honor roll in high school, but they also never saw her on an inmate roll in jail. And then they watched her graduate from NYU on the only timetable that really works—their child's, not their own.

So don't stand and rage at Mother Nature's waters, but don't think that there's nothing you can do. Take her measure and then decide how to best redirect her tides. These things take time and thought to do well. Most of all, they require the persistence and patience of love.

Cheats

"You know, Dad, they cheat at West Point too."

The What

DO

- Keep your cool—*what you see is not what your teen sees.*
- Know that cheating is now the *norm*, not the exception. (*Fifty to 80 percent* of kids cheat.)
- Know that many kids see cheating as an accepted academic tool.
- Be worried, not furious. Your worry might inspire him to learn a value; your fury will inspire him to learn to cheat better.
- Be sure *you* didn't foster this (with excessive pressure, by poor example, or by doing his work for him). If you did, clean up your mess. (See "Apologize, Won't," Part 2.)
- *Calmly* ask for your teen's reasons for cheating.
- Look to help him according to his *reasons*, not to punish him according to your anger.
- Ask your kid to think and write about any downsides of cheating.
- Ask him which feels better: a hard-won C or a stolen A; when he says "the A," ask what that A would give him and what that C *could* give him.
- Tell him that you'd be very sad about that A and very proud of that C. And be sure that's true.

- Insist that he 'fess up about his actions and try to make it right with the teacher.
- See a helper if your teen cheats repeatedly. (See "Getting Help," Part 9.)

DON'T

- Yell. Your screaming lets him off the hook by putting the focus on *your* behavior, not his.
- Just accept this as "normal." It might be, but it's hurting him.
- Push grades over effort.
- Model cheating, or you'll have no right to criticize his.
- Punish for a first offense. Punishing won't fix this. (See "Parenting Teenagers," Part 9.)
- Give him answers to force *your* values; instead, give him questions to help him find *his own*.

The Why

Academic cheating has grown over the past thirty years to a point where most of today's adolescents not only admit to cheating but think it's not really, well, *cheating*. Some experts worry that this attitude is a result of the adult culture's love of cutthroat, win-at-all-cost "competition" that prizes outcome over effort: "Winning isn't everything—it's the only thing," and "There's first place—and then there's everyone else." These "just do whatever it takes" messages have even permeated sports, the one arena where values such as honor, fairness, and 100 percent effort used to be celebrated along with the winning. Contemporary sports have now largely become a process of segregating people as "winners" or "losers" with the participants deciding that *any* behavior that promotes winning is OK (taking performance-enhancing drugs, stealing the opposition's signals, and so on) and seeing "winners" as more worthwhile human beings than "losers." In business, sports, and even relationships adults often use combat metaphors that justify any means to the end of victory. It's no longer enough to just play hard and savor the challenge and joy of competition. Now you must "crush" your opponent, "bring him to his knees," or "blow him away."

With these adult messages ringing in their ears, why in the world would teens not cheat? They'd be crazy to give up a competitive advantage such as that, especially when they encounter obstacles. (You know, those things that used to be viewed as character- and resilience-building opportunities.) Thus, predictably, kids report that they cheat most often if (1) they're struggling (usually in math and science classes), (2) they feel overpressured (by parents, peers, teachers, or themselves), or (3) their parents have too often done too much of their work. If you see those factors in your child, chat with him about this temptation even if cheating has not yet occurred. I guarantee that the world is telling him that being a "loser" (failing even with honest effort) is a fate worse than death and that cheating is bad only if you get caught.

Your parental calmness is key in responding here, so take time to chill before opening your mouth to your child. That control effort is well worth the doing since cheating is an issue with impact far beyond the stealing of grades. It has to do with very critical teen beliefs about things such as self-worth, trust, and resilience. These are issues that strike at the very heart of your kid's number one teenage task: *figuring out who he is*. (See "Identity," Part 9.)

The How

To get calm, first understand that to your kid's eye *everybody cheats*, or so it seems. Very successful presidents, preachers, principals, police officers, and professional football coaches have very publicly been found to betray, lie, test-rig, frame, and illegally videotape to get what they want in a fashion easier than playing by the rules. So your kid might just be learning the "secrets to success" as presented to him by "exemplary" adult leaders.

Your job, as always, is to get past trying only to control your teen's behavior and instead getting at the *beliefs* that drive those behaviors. (See "Parenting Teenagers," Part 9.) Do that with quiet questions, first about why he cheated and then about the real costs of cheating, such as his self-worth ("Does self-esteem come from hard effort or easy outcome?"), his honor ("Is honor about what you do when people are looking or when they are not?"), and his resilience to attack the rest of his life ("Are we stronger after getting a full-effort C or a stolen A?"). If he continues the behavior, take increasingly invasive steps to stop it (restrict computer use, insist on supervised testing, and so on) and see a helper ASAP since bigger things might be involved. (See "Getting Help," Part 9.) But for the first offense, take your time to talk this out in ways that make your kid think more about his values and less about his parents' anger. Help him learn that, in the end, the cheater who wins the game loses by a terrible margin. He loses himself.

WANT TO LEARN MORE?

Psychology of Academic Cheating, by Eric M. Anderman (Academic Press, 2006)

Homework, Won't Do

"Homework is irrelevant to my lifestyle."

—BRIANNA, AGE THIRTEEN

The What

DO

- Stay calm. There are countless other parents who wish their worst teen problem was homework.
- Know that Mother Nature has safety nets for kids who boot high school (called community colleges).
- View your teen's avoidance as a *symptom*, not a *sin*.
- Know that most homework avoiders are not happy campers and most homework doers are.
- Know that somewhere inside of your kid a doer is hiding.
- Try to figure out what keeps your doer away from her desk (fear, depression, learning/organization problem, poor workspace, anger, and so on).
- Offer to help or, better yet, to get her help. (We adults are amazingly more effective with *other* people's kids.)
- Consider offering incentives that can also become consequences, such as earning (or not earning) computer time, money, and so on. (See "Bribes/Incentives," Part 9.)

DON'T

- Yell, nag, or threaten. (As you've seen, those tricks never work.)
- Fight bitterly over homework. (You can win a battle and lose a war.)
- Just quit. Your continued calm concern will take root one day.
- Do homework for your teen. (That only makes her feel worse.)

The Why

You must stay cool, or your rage can trigger power and control struggles and give your child additional reasons not to do her homework. Plus, your anger and her subsequent feelings of rejection can lead you to be reading other sections of this book about crises far worse than homework. All kids want to achieve, so view your teen's reluctance as a sign of another problem you must ferret out and then try to remedy. For example, what parents often see as "lazy" is just a cover for kids who think it's less painful to flunk themselves (by not trying) than to get flunked after having tried. But just like that baseball player who's too scared to get up to bat, your kid will never see if she can get a hit until she takes some swings. And you never know what kind of coaching she needs until someone analyzes her swing. So your immediate goal is to get your kid into that batter's box, not to get a hit but just to take a few swings.

The How

First, stop doing all you've likely been doing (yelling, threatening, nagging), and apologize for having made her feel worse. Get yourself calm by knowing that lots of kids who lose their potential in high school find it in college (and community colleges are great places to learn how to learn). Then use Dr. Fred Hanna's subpersonality trick where you hook the adult/doer part of him. ("Nicki, I hear you when you say that you hate homework and will never, ever do it. I know that's what most of you feels. But is there a small part of you, perhaps just a 5 percent part, that thinks maybe you should do homework? Yes? OK, can I talk to that Nicki for a minute?") Ask that "doer" kid why she thinks *she* should do her homework, and keep asking until you get answers reflecting *her own* belief system, not yours. ("Why do *you* think that homework might be good for *your* life?") Once she admits that she wants to do well for her, propose some of the steps noted earlier to help her to get at her real avoidance issue.

Ask the "doer" part of your teen to push hard only for a short time, perhaps four weeks, just to see how she feels after trying. This helps her task looks less daunting than a total life commitment, and often after two weeks of trying her good feelings about doing her job will keep her keepin' on. If you offer incentives, be sure they reward her *effort* (time and energy) and not her outcome (grades). Finally, set up a meeting for you, your teen, and her teachers to jointly discuss what needs to be done (tutoring, educational testing, doing homework at school, and so on).

If her homework performance stays spotty, see a helper, but don't yell or nag. But don't quit on your child either. Softly revisit (not nag about) this issue with her from time to time since time is on your side. (See "Adolescent Brain Development," and "Adolescent Psychological Development," Part 9.) Tell her you're always there to help her if/when she decides it's time to get out of the dugout and take a shot in the batter's box. Quietly remind her that no one in the history of the game ever got a hit without stepping into that box.

WANT TO LEARN MORE?

The Homework Myth, by Alfie Kohn (Da Capo Lifelong Books, 2006)

Yes, Your Parents ARE Crazy! by Michael J. Bradley (Harbor Press, 2004)

School, Refuses to Go

"I swear I'll go tomorrow . . . tomorrow . . . tomorrow."

The What

DO

- Stay cool. Yelling and threatening will pull your teen's bed covers up even higher.
- Share some tea and calmly probe his reason for refusing to go. A "catch up on sleep day" might be OK; an "anxiety day" can never be.
- Know that every consecutive "anxiety day" absence increases the odds of *permanent* absence.
- Insist on *some* in-school time, even if just to sit in the counselor's office.
- Know that once inside that door your teen will likely be fine.
- Immediately get him to a helper and push hard for a same-day appointment. (See "Getting Help," Chapter 9.)

DON'T

- Use fear to fight fear. Your anger will only feed your child's anxiety.
- Think that your teen can beat his fear by bagging school.
- Just brush off his request without listening well. (See "Communication/Empathy," Part 9.)
- Underestimate how scary school might be for your teenager.
- Underestimate how crippling this fear can become if his fears come to rule his choices.

The Why

Most kids want to bag school at some point in their careers, but the key to your response is figuring out what is at the root of your teen's request. If you're thinking of giving him a "mental health day," almost any reason is OK except, ironically, fear/anxiety. That's when you must work the hardest to get his "face in the place" since fear grows exponentially with every day we give to it. (Think about negotiating with terrorists and you'll get the idea.) Conversely, once your kid gets into that building, his fear will likely begin to diminish quickly. So pull out all the stops to get him there if at all possible, and yes, this is a situation that warrants your missing your own obligations since allowing him a "fear day" could be the start of a "fear year" or worse.

The How

After canceling your own morning, allow your teen to talk about why he doesn't want to face his own. Hold him close and tell him you can see that this is very hard for him. Ask if he can identify a *specific* reason for his fear, then ask him if that thing is a *horror* (like 9/11) or a *frustration* (like jerks). This is a therapy exercise to help that teen brain to get some perspective and control over his fear. Explain to him how mere frustrations can paralyze us if we don't stand up to them and that his terrible, anxious feeling will grow worse if he lets it call his shots but will shrink if he can push through it.

Be supportive but firm, telling him that he must face his fear or it might come to own him. Give ground very slowly if he's really dug in, but keep that dialogue running about the consequences of conceding to fear. Softly remind him that the law *requires* him to attend school (his is *not* a volunteer army) and that you love him far too much to bail him out with a note citing a phony illness that could morph into a real one. Offer generous antianxiety incentives (bribes) since this is a high-stakes game. Suggest that you can pick him up early if he doesn't feel better after attending the morning. At the very least, insist on some form of him being in school, even if just to be in the counselor's office. (Call ahead—the counselor should know this drill very well.) Be sure to make clear the fact that missing school for fear equates to serious illness—no other "play" privileges (friends, computers, phones) can be had until he recovers. If you hit a brick wall, get on the phone to helpers and press to have him seen immediately if at all possible. Some helpers keep slots open for such emergencies since they know how quickly school avoidance can snowball.

Finally, if he makes it to school that day, ask him that night about how he feels having faced up to his anxiety. Ask how he feels having refused to negotiate with that terrorist named fear.

Underachieves

"I like to work down to my potential."

The What

DO

- Stay calm. More parental anger = less teen achievement.
- View poor achievement as a *skill* issue, not a *character* flaw.
- Ask if *she* really wants to do better and *why*. Then make this a joint effort. (See introductory text earlier in Part 5.)
- Join with the school staff in looking for possible causes (learning challenges, poor sleep/nutrition, disorganization, anxiety, peer influence, and so on).
- Offer (don't force) nightly homework assistance from you or a tutor.
- Suggest that she try doing homework at the library.
- Set up a quiet, uncluttered, and well-lit homework space *without* electronics.
- Ask for only a two-week experiment to see how doing assignments works/feels.
- "Chunk" homework into twenty- to thirty-minute efforts with movement breaks.

- Offer incentives based on her *effort*, not on her grades. (See "Bribes/Incentives," Part 9.)
- See a helper. (See "Getting Help," Part 9.)
- Calmly stay at this. One day your teen will "get it" if you don't "lose it."

DON'T

- Go to war over grades. (You may lose more than you win.)
- Just accept her mediocre efforts without quietly but continually questioning them.
- Get panicked. Many, many kids lose academic motivation in high school and find it in community college.

The Why

Your first task is to get your own anger and frustration in hand before you deal with hers. Your upset will only provide an easy diversion to fight over, enabling your kid to avoid taking a hard, painful look at herself. Try seeing academic skills as tennis skills: they both take lots of practice, coaching, and effort, but neither can really be angrily forced—*your kid has to want to do this*. So go back to square one with her to find *her* belief about *why* she should do well academically: "Honey, what's the point of your going to school? What's the payoff for *you?*" Once you establish *her* rationale for doing school, join forces with her to help her to get to *her* goal, not yours. For without her involvement and commitment, even your loving efforts might feel like anger and control and only make things worse.

The How

Your child's possible reasons for doing poorly are many and often complex, so get the experts involved if her poor academic achievement becomes a long-term problem. Get the school personnel (teachers, counselors, school psychologists, and so on) together in joint meetings where everyone, *including your child*, brainstorms to find solutions. (Bring food—those staff really appreciate that.) Homework is typically a key part of the problem, so try the suggestions noted earlier regardless of your kid's specific challenges. If all of your best efforts seem to hit brick walls, don't despair and go nuts, but don't go away either. Remember that your parenting mission is not to control your child but to *teach her to control herself*. (See "Parenting Teenagers," Part 9.) In that light, as parents of teenagers we are in the failure business. We are here to help our kids learn powerful lessons from their failures to help them eventually succeed with themselves: "Hey Mom—I just discovered something. I actually can't study with my TV, computer, phone, and iPod all running. Do you think that scientists have discovered this yet?" Beyond all else, do not let grade worries become family wars where you lose your connections with your kid.

Her grades are important, but they are a secondary concern. Your priority is keeping close to her heart, through the As *and* the Fs. She can always make up for bad grades later in life. Lost love is gone forever.

WANT TO LEARN MORE?

You Can Do It: How to Boost Your Child's Achievement in School, by Michael E. Bernard (Grand Central Publishing, 1997)

PART 6

SERIOUS ISSUES

IF YOU'VE ARRIVED at this part of the book, you'll find no jokes here. I know they'd only feel insulting. The situations discussed in this section are terrible—these are the times when we parents learn how incredibly vulnerable and helpless we can become through the trials of our children. That's one feeling that nonparents are fortunate never to know.

Dad sat silently stunned for the longest moment, a reaction so extraordinarily rare that his wife and his twenty-year-old son were frozen, able only to stare at him. They seemed to have almost stopped breathing. That's when I realized that Dad was the one fighting to get his breath. "I . . . feel like . . . like I can't breathe," he gasped.

Dad was a man who looked like he could never be over-whelmed by anything. An ex-wrestler, ex-Marine, even in middle age his chiseled body was still a study in strength and discipline. Not the screaming, aggressive, in-your-face power, but that quiet, steely, move-you-with-a-gaze kind of tenacity. He had no tattoos, no muscle shirt, no chains or spikes. He needed none.

When finally he got a breath, he leaned forward, sank his face into his powerful hands, and made a noise that his family had clearly never heard before. He was softly crying. "I . . . don't, I . . . can't," he stammered. After another long pause, he lifted his head and seemed to speak to his hands, talking so softly that no one moved a muscle so that we could listen in. "All my life," he began, "it's been about challenges. I was a 'loser' when I was a teenager. Then I learned that no matter the obstacle, no mat-ter the odds, if you're willing to work harder than your enemy, to endure more than your enemy, to persevere longer than your enemy, you will prevail. This has been the center of my life, this belief. Even through those terrible three years of fighting my son's addiction, the overdose and all, I knew . . . *I knew* that we would win this. And now, to hear that . . . after thirteen months clean . . ." Dad's voice trailed off, and his face found his hands again. Now he cried hard.

"I feel so . . . so . . ." Here he looked up at me in amazement, as if feeling something for the first time in his fifty-two years of life. "I feel *helpless*. I am actually *powerless* over this. There is *nothing* that I can do to save my son's life. I would run through a minefield to save him. I would take a bullet for him and die a happy man, happy in knowing that I did *something* to help this kid that I love so much. But this, this . . . *horror* . . . all I can do is sit . . . and cry, like a child. Of all the challenges I've faced, of all those enemies—*flowers . . . poppies*—turn out to be what puts me on my knees. How do you fight with flowers for the life of your son?"

The father just sat and wept. The son had just confessed to relapsing in his struggle with heroin.

I didn't insult you with insensitive humor, but I might anger you by offering hope, a luxury that you might feel your family cannot afford right now because the future seems so ominous and you feel so helpless. Like that father, many of us believe that hope makes future failure more painful. But that dad could not see what you likely cannot see: the face of a teenager, confronting some terrible crisis suddenly inspired by the simple, quiet declaration of love of a parent for a child. That love can bring hope to a hopeless adolescent, and that can save his life. But it needs to be offered in the right way.

When that dad was crying, I watched the son watch the father. That boy saw a whole new dimension of his dad open up to him, a part ten times more helpful than the father's awesome personal power and determination. The son had heard all of Dad's hopeful "Winners never quit, and quitters never win" pep talks. Although they were all offered in love, they all just made the son feel less loved. After all, if you believe you're a loser, then what can be more distancing than the peppy bumper stickers of those who never lose? But, when the all-time winner breaks down and cries, admits to feeling hopeless and helpless, feels like a *loser* because he *can't save someone he loves*, well, helpless and hopeless is something the child can identify with. And the child starts to think that if the winner can sometimes feel like a loser, then perhaps, just maybe, losers can become winners. That's called *hope*. When that admission comes in the same breath with the unconditional love, it can become the inspiration to try to battle heroin once again.

In that moment Dad's power was not in his *strength* but in his *weakness*. When the son saw the father as vulnerable, he was able to relate to him, to connect with him, to listen to him, to be inspired by him. The same is true for our own children with us, and it is precisely those things that can save their lives. But there are a few other tools you should have.

In the following topics you'll find some initial strategies specific to each crisis to keep your kid safe until you can get to the expert help you will need. There are a few tricks that work well with each of these crises. First, know that your kid likely knows what he *should* do; it's just the *doing it* part that's hard. So telling him the obvious usually helps very little and often hurts very much: "You've got to stop these suicidal thoughts!" Second, yelling that advice hurts even more: "Goddamnit!! What the hell's the matter with you? Are you just looking for attention? You've got a great life. Stop talking about wanting to die!!"

What approach does help? Going in softly, sharing your own past failures and frailties: "Son, I'm so sorry that you feel so bad. I've also had a few times where I didn't want to live, where I thought nothing would ever get better. For me that was a terrible feeling. Can you tell me about yours?" Regardless of your particular crisis, the advice to hold your advice will serve you well. Because in virtually every piece of research regarding every terrible thing that can happen to your teen, it turns out that loving connections with parents is the number-one factor we find in successful prevention *and* recovery efforts. Then, only after making that loving connection, calmly but firmly insist that the *family as a team* get expert help to fight the monster that's coming after your kid.

So leave the advice giving to the docs, your anger to your punching bag, and instead dose your kid with the most powerful medicine that anyone can give: the love of a "winner" parent offering the hope of an ex-teenage "loser."

Abused, May Have Been Sexually

"Children's bodies aren't like automobiles with the assailant's fingerprints lingering on the wheel. The world of sexual abuse is quintessentially secret. It is the perfect crime."

—BEATRIX CAMPBELL

The What

DO

- Find the strength to stay calm and reassuring. (Just do it.)
- Take your child's word about the event unless proven otherwise.
- Know that almost all abuse victims are assaulted by someone they know and often trust.
- Remove the alleged abuser from any contact with your kid.
- Report all claims to the authorities immediately.
- Get an immediate medical evaluation, especially if the event is within forty-eight hours.
- See a helper ASAP. (See "Getting Help," Part 9.)
- Repeatedly assure her that none of this is her fault even if she did not resist or fight back.
- Stay very close with your child until treatment has begun.

DON'T

- Dismiss any claim, even if it sounds far-fetched.
- Make your teen confront her abuser to "get to the truth."
- React with shock, rage, or horror (even though you want to scream).

- Share the story with anyone except those who need to know (parents, police officers, doctors).
- Think or talk about revenge. Your job is to heal your child, not to hunt her abuser.

The Why

Hearing a child say that she has been abused is so terribly shocking to parents that often we respond with disbelief and denial. We hate thinking that this stuff really happens, but the numbers of confirmed cases are near epidemic levels. Even more shocking is the fact that few abuse reports are declared false (perhaps 10 percent of sexual abuse cases are dismissed as contrived), and many more reports simply cannot be substantiated as either real or contrived.

Your initial response to your child is a key factor in determining how well and how quickly she will recover from the trauma. Parental reactions of doubt, horror, rage, or hysteria will increase your teen's existing feelings of shame, loss of trust, fear, and self-loathing. If she sees any shift in how you used to act with her, she'll assume that she's now less of a person in your eyes. That can be deadly. Conversely, staying calm, quiet, and lovingly supportive will help her hope and believe that she will recover and that she is still the person that she always was.

Become your teen's shadow at least until you guys get to see a helper for an evaluation, since suicide can appear to be a good remedy for overwhelming pain. Other than the "need to know" people, tell *no one* else about the abuse without your teen's consent. That list includes siblings, relatives, family friends, and so on. She *and only she* must be the one to decide when and whom to tell. Abuse is the ultimate lack of control, and your kid needs to feel as much control as you can provide.

Never talk about revenge, as much as you might want to. Your child has had enough violence for a lifetime, and thinking about more will only make her feel worse. She desperately needs quiet healing, and vigilante talk will only worsen her pain.

The How

If there ever are times for parents to "be the rock," this is one. In those first few days after reporting abuse, your teen will orient herself according to your reaction. She will need to unload her pain on you and not have to worry about yours. Listen better than you ever have. (See "Communication/Empathy," Part 9.) You simply must dig down and find the strength to be strong. Beyond all else, be sure you don't fall into the destructive belief that young teens can somehow consent to having sex with adults and that your child might be partially responsible for the event. Even if she "consented" to the act, any adult who engaged with her is a manipulative predator who took unfair advantage.

If you have any suspicions that something may have happened to your kid that she's not telling you, you must check them out. Some symptoms of unreported abuse are anxiety, depression, nightmares, aggression, and sexual acting out. The best approach is to preface a conversation by saying how much you love her, that even as a teen she is *still a child* and thus cannot be "bad," and that nothing, *nothing* can change any of that. Then just ask straight out. If she pauses, or denies in a way that alerts your parental instincts, suggest that she chat with a "caring stranger." (See "Getting Help," Part 9.) In abuse cases female helpers are often the easiest folks for your child to quickly trust since most abusers are male.

WANT TO LEARN MORE?

How Long Does It Hurt: A Guide to Recovering from Incest and Sexual Abuse for Teenagers, Their Friends, and Their Families, by Cynthia L. Mather (Jossey-Bass, 2004)

Anorexia/ Bulimia, Has

"When it comes to adolescent eating disorders, it is usually the parents' responsibility to seek help. The girl with the eating disorder is often the last to know she is ill."

—AMY BAKER

The What

DO

- Know anorexia's symptoms: obsessive exercise, eating little, not eating with others, loss of at least 10 percent of body weight, loss of menstruation, seeing a "disgustingly fat" self in her "skinny" reflection.
- Know bulimia's clues: missing food, hidden wrappers, tooth decay, vomiting signs, disappearing after meals, scarred/cut fingers (teeth wounds to gag-inducing fingers), irregular periods, and secret laxative use/diarrhea.
- Know that bulimics can maintain average weight and appear to eat normally in public.
- Know that kids with eating disorders are great at hiding, denying, and explaining them away—*even to themselves.*
- Know that their families can sometimes be "great" at that as well.

- Know that these kids hide tremendous guilt and shame under a Kevlar cloak of denial.
- Move very softly and gently when confronting and frame your teen's behavior as a *symptom*, not a *sin*.
- Appear as calm and nonjudgmental as possible to reduce her feelings of guilt and shame.
- Calmly but firmly insist on an immediate visit to your kid's physician for a full workup since these disorders can kill (plus she might be better able to confide there).
- Keep calmly revisiting this issue until your child agrees to gets help. (See "Getting Help," Part 9.)
- If repeated attempts fail, consult with your local mental health authorities on having her forcibly committed into treatment. *This is a traumatic, last-resort option.*
- Go immediately to the ER if you see possible extreme symptoms (weakness, dizziness, chest pain, irregular breathing, fainting, seizures, and so on).

DON'T

- Think that boys can't suffer with eating disorders as well. Increasingly, they do.
- Ridicule, yell, criticize, demand, or plead. (The best approach is the quietest and least emotional.)
- "Advise" or coach your teen. (No, she can't *"just stop it."*)
- Think that your teen can beat this on her own (no matter what she says).
- Allow this to go on without confronting it.

The Why

An eating disorder is one if those things that just can't be grasped fully by those who haven't suffered one. To unaffected folks it seems so simple to "just eat, for God's sake," or to "just stop eating, for God's sake." Thus these behaviors can seem like willful, self-centered acts of vanity or excuses to eat whatever we want. The fact is that these food urges are among the most powerful and irresistible that anyone can experience. For example, an anorexic girl who stands in front of a mirror can *actually see* a "disgustingly fat pig" while looking at the *very same reflection* that others see as a gaunt, skeletal girl. This stuff is way beyond vanity or lack of discipline. Because of the terrible power of eating disorders, parents must move very skillfully in getting that child to the expert help she needs. And that help will help much more if she agrees to get it instead of being coerced (which you will have to do if all else fails).

The How

The drill is to make a loving, caring connection before you get to the tough part where your teenager must acknowledge needing help. Your kid is likely feeling very out of control right now, so do not appear to be controlling, but rather show her a way to take control of herself (by getting help). Your tone should be calm, reassuring, nonjudgmental, and matter-of-fact, and the setting should be private, where no one else can overhear: "Honey, please just hear me out for two minutes without responding. It's very clear that food is very painful for you. Please know that there are people who can help us [note that word *us*] with this. Eating disorders are not about weak or strong, good or bad; they're just like diabetes or asthma. No one beats them alone. I'm sorry for making you upset, and I hate intruding into your business, but I love you way too much to just watch you struggle so terribly. Please don't feel as if you need to say anything right now. We'll talk again tomorrow." Let that soak in a bit and then softly follow up as many times as it takes. Use Dr. Fred Hanna's subpersonality trick, where you say, "Sweetie, I hear you saying that you have no food issues. But is there a small part, perhaps a 2 percent part, that worries that you might? Yes? OK, then can I talk with that 2 percent part for a minute?" Treatment works much better when the treated agree to get help. Go to the forcible commitment option only as a last resort, if you're getting nowhere and you see your teen's health seriously deteriorating. In most areas, having a teen committed means having her taken into custody by the police, restrained as needed, and transported to the nearest ER, where she will spend many angry and uncomfortable hours or even days before getting to specialized treatment. Although you may need to take this drastic action, that kind of power typically works great in the short term and lousy in the long. There is another power that works great in the long term but looks lousy in the short. That's the love of a parent, not the handcuffs of a cop. Your quietly expressed love will eventually be heard by the small, frightened voice inside of your child that desperately needs *and wants* your help, regardless of what she says.

WANT TO LEARN MORE?

Help Your Teenager Beat an Eating Disorder, by James Lock and Daniel le Grange (Guilford Press, 2005)

Helping Your Troubled Teen: Learn to Recognize, Understand, and Address the Destructive Behavior of Today's Teens and Preteens, by Cynthia Kaplan, Blaise Aguirre, and Michael Rater (Fair Winds Press, 2007)

Drugs/Alcohol, Uses Excessively

"I don't have a drug problem. I can stop anytime I want to. I just never want to."

—ERIC, AGE FIFTEEN

The What

DO

- Know that alcohol *is a drug*—and a particularly dangerous one for teens.
- Know that marijuana *is a drug* and that today's version is much more potent and damaging than your "back in the day" weed.
- Know that a prescription pill *is a drug* and can be as addicting and dangerous as heroin.
- Know that teen brains are much more prone to addiction than adult brains.
- Know that heavy drug use can distort your teen's thinking to a point where *you must think for him.*
- Quietly confront your kid, saying that his use is out of control and that he must accept immediate help. (See "Getting Help," Part 9.)
- Get an immediate evaluation at a rehab/detoxification facility. If none are available and your child is sick/impaired, immediately go to a physician or emergency room (ER) to be sure that he's physically safe for the time being.
- If he refuses help and insists on continued heavy use:
  - Get his car keys, money, and wallet (but *no* wrestling matches).

- Confront him *calmly* but *firmly*. ("We know that you are using drugs. We love you and will take care of you, and you will be OK, but you must do exactly what we say. You will stay in the house for now.")
- Call a rehabilitation/detoxification facility for an immediate evaluation.
- If your kid is sick/impaired, and no help is immediately available, go to the nearest ER.
- Call his friends *and* their parents. ("Our son has a serious drug problem. If you care about him, please *do not* give him any money under any circumstances.")
- Search his belongings to determine what additional drugs he might be using.
- Watch him twenty-four/seven until you get help, but do not physically restrain him if he bolts.
- If all else fails, consider "rehab-by-cop." (See "The How," following.)

DON'T

- Yell, cry, lecture, or ask questions like, "Why are you doing this?" or "Don't you know that this can kill you?"
- Threaten your teen. ("If you don't stop this, you're out of this house.")
- Accept any promises that postpone his getting help. ("I swear I'll stop this time if you don't send me to rehab.") Without treatment, the best predictor of your teen's future is his past.
- Allow your kid to leave the house. ("Son, if you leave, we will call the police, and then you might be detoxing in a cell. Neither of us want that.")
- Attempt to detox your teen at home or to just let him "sleep it off." (He might not wake up.)

The Why

Frequent use of *any* drug is a terrible threat to teenagers. Their developing brains don't have adult defenses against the toxic and addictive effects of drugs. For example, teens who start to drink at age fourteen are *five times* more likely to become addicts than those who start at twenty-one. (See "Adolescent Brain Development," Part 9.)

Some poisons, such as heroin, can kill them quickly. Others, like booze and weed, usually won't destroy them fast but like a lamprey will slowly suck their life energy until using becomes the only thing they really care about. These "soft" drugs may be the most damaging of all because so many of us adults do them ourselves, and thus we sort of wink at their use by our kids. (One-third of alcohol illegally provided to our children is handed to them by their *parents*.) Most teens who use won't overdose or become addicts. Many will. There are some factors that increase the odds of addiction (genetics, parental use, peer use), but there is really no way of knowing which kid is using "safely." *Thus we parents cannot play Russian roulette with the lives of our children by ignoring their frequent, heavy drug use.*

Loving drug-involved children means loving them enough to firmly confront them with quiet words that often lead to their screaming threats: "If you send me to rehab, I'll hate you forever." To which we must respond, "That would truly break my heart. But I love you enough to lose your love if that is what gives you your life."

The How

Many folks believe that forcing kids into drug treatment is ineffective, that teens must truly want to be there to benefit. But, perhaps surprisingly, the relapse rate for the "volunteers" is about the same as it is for the "draftees," which suggests that coerced drug treatment works about as well as elective. So your mission is to get your heavily-drug-involved adolescent into treatment *willingly if possible* (since that's less traumatic) but in any way it takes. Your first move is to simply ask: "Son, it's clear that your use is out of control. Are you ready to get help?" Your second is to assume control by "telling" him that this is the way it has to be. (See "The What," preceding.) This works more often than you'd think, appealing to that "smart" part of his brain that knows that he's in terrible danger. Failing that, be aware that it's nearly impossible to legally force your child into rehab on your own. (Check with your local authorities on this.) However, a *juvenile court* can and usually does mandate treatment (not jail) for a minor's first drug offense.

So should you turn your kid in to the police for illegal drug use? Take a look at your local juvenile justice system to help you to decide about that huge risk. If that program seems more about helping kids than hurting them, give it some thought. Given the excellent cops and courts in my own town, I'd rat out my drug-involved, treatment-resistant child in a New York minute.

WANT TO LEARN MORE?

Helping Your Troubled Teen: Learn to Recognize, Understand, and Address the Destructive Behavior of Today's Teens and Preteen, by Cynthia Kaplan, Blaise Aguirre, and Michael Rater (Fair Winds Press, 2007)

Lost and Found: A Mother and Son Find Victory Over Teen Drug Addiction, by Christy Crandell (Pascoe Publishing, 2006)

Pregnant, Becomes

"It was after I had my child that I saw that I was still a child."

—SUSAN, AGE FIFTEEN

This section speaks to the needs of a pregnant girl since this is a problem that impacts her life far more than the boy's; however, the father's parents should review this section as well to help him and them define his role as *supporting* the girl in her decisions and not imposing his views on her. Further, please understand that this section reviews only the *psychological* aspects of this crisis and not any accompanying religious/moral issues that must also be considered.

The What

DO

- Get your emotions in hand before opening your mouth. Yelling, crying, or commanding will only make things worse—*and, yes, they can get much worse.*
- Reassure your teen that you love her and will stand by her to help her to sort this out.
- Have a doctor confirm the pregnancy and get an estimate of duration.
- Ask your daughter to forgo any drug/alcohol use.
- Know that there is no painless solution here, only less painful ones.
- Get a helper involved ASAP to guide the family through this critical time. (See "Getting Help," Part 9.)

DON'T

- Give your teen morality lectures. She's already pregnant. Your time now must be devoted exclusively to making sure that her next decision will be better than her last.
- Make her feel more scared, ashamed, or worthless than she likely already does. (This will only encourage more bad decisions.)
- Celebrate this as a milestone event. (Pregnancy for a teenager is not an accomplishment; it's a car wreck.)
- Mandate solutions. ("You will raise this baby" or "You will have an abortion.") She must work this through to find her best option.
- See teen marriage as a viable choice. She might be more likely to be abducted by Martians than to have a successful marriage. (See "The Why," following.)
- Rely on the promises of a teen father in making a decision. (No matter what he says, those Martians will have abducted him within a year.)
- Overlook the adoption option. This rarely used choice can offer a workable alternative to the abort-or-raise dilemma.

The Why

The data on teen pregnancy show why it is the crisis that can bring worse crises. So these must be reviewed carefully as part of the decision process. Your daughter's predictions of "Oh, that won't happen to me" should be met with calm responses of "How are you different from these other girls?" and "Do you think that any of these girls ever thought that any of these terrible things would happen to them?" Things such as:

- Divorce: 90 percent of pregnancy-based teen marriages break up within two years.
- Abandonment: 80 percent of teen mothers receive 0 percent of dollars promised by the fathers. (But they do get lots of promises.)
- Crushing poverty: most teen mothers never complete high school and live out their lives looking up at the poverty line.
- Traumatized babies: children raised by teen mothers are exponentially more likely to end up homeless, to be raised in foster homes, to be abused and/or neglected, and to have serious behavioral/learning problems.

Your family's enemy is that frightening, fairy-tale, everything-will-work-out thinking that seems to overtake girls *and* boys *and far too many of their parents* in the face of a surprise adolescent pregnancy. Warm fairy tales are best chilled with cold data presented dispassionately but consistently by adults who know the realities of raising children. Your job is to present that information in a way that helps your daughter make a good decision based on reality, not fantasy.

The How

Veteran parents who've preceded you down this teen crisis path say it's much like getting blindsided by a speeding truck. One moment you're cruising along, happily humming some oldies tune, when suddenly you find yourself upside down in a smoldering car wreck, fighting to get your breath and wondering what the hell happened. The thought of your child having a child is so incomprehensible that it instantly throws everything around your family into a spin. The plans, the hopes, the dreams—everything suddenly seems changed in a terrible, out-of-control way.

And while control is exactly the thing you need to regain, be sure to go for that quiet, rational decision-making control and not the "You'll do what I tell you!" type since the stakes may never be higher for your kid.

First, do nothing except to reassure your terrified child that she is still your daughter, she is still loved, and you will all get through this as a family. Then get *yourself* under control by calling a time-out to collect your own thoughts before you start to help her with hers. This is another "parent medal of honor" moment where you must act superhuman while feeling all too human. If you think that yelling at her will help, picture a cop yelling at an injured driver trapped in a smoking, wrecked car, moralizing about her lousy driving decisions. These are times for lifesaving efforts, not lectures.

Begin by asking to have the family hook up with a helper to begin collecting and considering information about teen pregnancy options. Together review all the data you can find. (See "The Why," preceding.) Then ask that you *all* discuss *all* of her options with her (abortion, adoption, and parenting) before she decides what she wants to do. Give her *questions*, not mandates, to help her realistically visualize the long-term realities: "What would raising a baby *really* be like for a sixteen-year-old?" If she has romantic visions of teen parenting, try writing out budgets based on her income potential, including child-care costs, since you must make it lovingly but firmly clear that this will be *her* child to raise, not yours. Next, suggest chatting with veteran teen moms to find out what their lives are like and even create a weekly planner showing what her daily life might look like *then* as opposed to now.

Finally, if your daughter ends up as so many teens do, terribly torn between two options she feels cannot work for her (parenting and aborting), don't forget the adoption option.

With so many wonderful adults desperately seeking babies, this makes so much sense for those terribly conflicted kids, although *only 4 percent* of pregnant teens choose this option. So consider having her meet with girls who found that adopting out was the best solution for them. This does take an amazing amount of vision and maturity, so be ready to lend her some.

Whatever her choice, it's critical that your daughter arrive calmly at that decision on her own but with your guidance. So before you impose any option on her, keep one fact in mind: *whatever the choice, she must live with it for the rest of her life.*

I know this all sounds so easy to say and so impossible to do, and it is exactly so. But if you can pull this off, you will find peace in your old age from your own past valor and in watching your adult daughter living a happy life because of a wise and thoughtful decision made during some very frightening days.

WANT TO LEARN MORE?

Kids Still Having Kids: Talking About Teen Pregnancy (Impact Books Series), by Janet Bode (Franklin Watts Publishers, 1999)

The Unplanned Pregnancy Book for Teens and College Students, by Dorrie Williams-Wheeler (Sparkledoll Productions, 2004)

Runs Away

"When I ran away I should have flown. 'Cause when my bus got to New York, all my problems had gotten there ahead of me."

—MARK, AGE SIXTEEN

The What

DO

- Know that one in seven teens runs away at least once.
- Know that running away is only a *symptom* of a larger, unsolved problem.
- Know that only half of the teens who bolt intend to leave forever (the "travelers"); the others expect to be back in their own beds in a day or two at most (the "sleepovers").
- Know that the travelers (particularly the younger ones) are at terrible risk for abuse, assault, and disease.
- Contact everyone to whom your teen might run to ask that he contact you as soon as he shows up. (A return call usually indicates a sleepover.) Tell them that you will *not* punish or drag your kid home. (Otherwise your *sleepover* might become a *traveler*.)
- If your teen calls:
  - Calmly sidestep the running away and say you'd like to work on the problem that caused him to run.
  - Allow him a day or two at a safe place to cool down and think.
  - Get to a helper to address his issue. (See "Getting Help," Part 9.)
- If you get no call, look for travel and destination clues:
  - Check your teen's hangouts, friends, phone/computer records, and room.
  - Call the police to request a "Lookout Alert."
  - Circulate a flyer with your kid's picture and your number.
  - Contact the National Center for Missing and Exploited Children at MissingKids.com.

DON'T

- Yell or punish for the running. (It's a *symptom*, not a *sin*.)
- Ever dare your child or "call his bluff" to run away.
- Tell your kid to stay out of your home. (He could die.)
- Call the police if you know he's in a safe place.
- Drag him home from a safe place. (He might just run farther the next time.)

The Why

Running away can feel like two very different things for a teen and his parents. What Mom and Dad often see as an in-your-face action is usually an "I don't know what else to do" *reaction* for a kid. Most teens are running from frustration and anger, many from abuse and neglect, but all are running *from* something, and most of those would rather not be running at all. What many parents see as a prohibited vacation, most teens experience as a highly stressful, uncomfortable, and often dangerous time. The one common thread among virtually all runaways is some family dysfunction, almost always a problem that is better resolved by treatment than by travel. Your first job is to contain your runaway at that safe sleepover level. ("Thanks so much for calling. We were very worried about you, and we want you to come home as soon as you feel ready. We love and miss you. We need to talk about getting some help for our family to find better ways to resolve our differences.") Don't issue demands, threats, challenges, or punishments or your teen will be checking that train schedule before he hangs up on you. The risks rise exponentially when he's buying tickets to ride.

The How

You've just got to get calm—and quickly. If it helps, know that your anger is literally life threatening to your child since it might send him off into the adolescent hell of "traveler" runaways (rape, prostitution, assault, drug use, disease, and so on). Neither of you wants that, and it doesn't have to happen *IF* you can get a message to your kid ASAP that does two things: reminds him that you love him, and opens a safer door for resolving his upset than the one on that bus. And the most powerful form of that message is an apology, one offered *especially* after he was so horrible to you: "Honey, I'm so sorry I yelled. I should have been able to keep my cool. I will try to do better the next time." (See "Apologize, Won't," Part 2.) Once he's safely home, call a time-out on the fight that set his feet in motion and get to that helper to work on the real issues here. (See "Getting Help," Part 9.) Fix that problem he's running from so that he can begin running toward the one thing he needs beyond all else and will never find anywhere else: *the love of his family.*

WANT TO LEARN MORE?

Helping Your Troubled Teen: Learn to Recognize, Understand, and Address the Destructive Behavior of Today's Teens and Preteens, by Cynthia Kaplan, Blaise Aguirre, and Michael Rater (Fair Winds Press, 2007)

Shoplifts

"It's not *really* stealing, you know."

—DARIEN, AGE TWELVE

The What

DO

- Stay calm. It's time to *teach*, not punish. (See "Parenting Teenagers," Part 9.)
- Understand that many kids truly don't see this as stealing, and almost half try it.
- Know that most teens shoplift to gain peer approval, not because they need anything.
- Know that most teens who *don't* do it have close relationships with their parents.
- Ask your teen how stealing made her feel. If she says "better," ask if there are better ways to feel "better."
- Ask if she would still say that shoplifting isn't really stealing if she owned that store.
- Ask what might happen if everyone thought that shoplifting was OK.
- Insist on restoration and apology for the theft.
- See a helper if this recurs. (See "Getting Help," Part 9.)

DON'T

- Go nuts. If you can stay calm, your teen's stealing gives you a great opportunity to teach about much more than shoplifting.
- Think this makes your child a true criminal (this just makes her a "crazy" teen).
- Blow it off. This could be a symptom of something more serious going on.
- Just punish her. She'll learn nothing but anger and may then want to steal more.

The Why

Shoplifting has become a fad among many teens, a behavior they describe as a harmless game, not as stealing. The problem is that often stealing can do many things that may help them feel much better. For example, some adolescents find that the thrill of that risk taking can boost their brain chemistry to help combat depression. This works so well that stealing can become addicting to some. (See "Adolescent Brain Development," Part 9.) But most kids steal primarily to gain status and acceptance from their peers. (Many steal items *for* their peers.) Thus the most common explanation for teen shoplifting is a need to boost poor self-esteem, that terribly misunderstood part of children that has gotten lots of bad press recently. (See "Self-Esteem, Has Poor," Part 3.) Political arguments aside, the fact is that self-worth drives teen behaviors as much as or more than any other aspect of their being, and theft is one scary example of that. So the odds are that your sticky-fingered child needs your help both with finding better ways of feeling better about herself and with expanding her moral development a tad.

The How

Resist your understandable urge to be outraged and offended or to punish your teen with groundings and such. Not only will that not teach her anything; it might actually increase her urges to steal again as soon as she can. Your best response is to use this incident to gift her with insight and a lifelong value, not a short-term wrist slap. First, with the preceding questions, help her understand her motivation to steal, and then help her think of better ways to fill those needs. (See "Risks, Takes Excessive," Part 2, and "Depression, May Have," Part 3.) If your teen can make that connection between her emotional needs and that behavior, she has a shot at changing it. Second, again with those earlier questions, get at her moral *beliefs* about stealing to help to develop her ethical code. The best method for both goals is to ask with questions versus lecture with answers. (See "Parenting Teenagers," Part 9.) Take lots of time with many breaks for her to sit and think or write out her thoughts. But as part of this process, be sure to include a trip back to the store (with you) to restore the theft and to apologize to the manager/owner (to be safe you might want to first contact the store to be sure that your teen won't be arrested if she 'fesses up). Your kid will resist this and will feel terribly embarrassed, but the right dose of shame turns out to be a great teaching tool. You might softly point out that it's interesting she's too ashamed to apologize to the owner if she truly thinks that shoplifting is no big deal. Tell her to watch out—she might actually be developing a conscience.

WANT TO LEARN MORE?

How to Talk so Teens Will Listen and Listen so Teens Will Talk, by Adele Faber and Elaine Mulish (Collins, 2006)

Suicidal, Is

"Suicide is a permanent solution to a temporary problem."

—PHIL DONAHUE

The What

DO

- Know the *Code Orange* factors (an increased risk for suicide):
  - Death of someone close (relative/peer)
  - Some teen-significant loss (failed relationship, rejection from college)

- Substance abuse (especially alcohol)
- Depression (See "Depression, May Have," Part 3.)
- Intense and prolonged anger
- Social isolation; feelings of worthlessness
- Know the *Code Red* factors (imminent risk):
  - Talking/writing about dying or hopeless "no way out" scenarios; sudden, unexplained happiness after a prolonged, deep depression
  - Withdrawing from activities, family, and friends
  - Giving away loved items
  - Presenting unusually poor appearance/hygiene
  - Having individual "good-bye" meetings with friends
  - Acquiring pills, guns, or ropes
  - Making "weak" or "attention-getting" attempts
- Get close and stay close to your kid.
- Use the "S" word directly. ("Have you thought about committing suicide?")
- Get your teen to a helper for an immediate evaluation. Stay with him twenty-four/seven (literally) until you get there. (See "Getting Help," Part 9.)
- Go to the nearest ER or crisis center if immediate help is not available.
- Remove all guns, pills, and ropes from the house. Check your kid's room and belongings for any hidden items.

DON'T

- Guess whether your teen is serious. If you're reading this, it *is* serious.
- Worry that asking about suicide will "put it in his head."
- Discount what he says. ("Oh you don't really want to die.")
- Brush off your child's pain. ("You'll feel better tomorrow.")
- Think that "weak" "attention-getting" attempts aren't dangerous.

- Assume he's OK if he "changes his mind" after talking with
  you. ("I'm so glad that you feel better, but the fact that you
  wanted to die means that we need to chat with a helper
  ASAP.")
- Think only depressed teens kill themselves. Many victims are
  angry adolescents giving the ultimate "screw you" to their
  worlds.

The Why

A fact disbelieved by many adults is that suicide among teenagers has roughly *tripled* since the mid-1970s. This disbelief causes
too many of us not to react to the warning signs as seriously as
we should. A child dying by his own hand is so unthinkable that
many of us minimize the thought, *even if he tells us about it.*
That's a fatal response since the majority of teens who commit
suicide do so shortly after telling someone that they want to die,
someone who didn't take them seriously enough (often a friend).
The tragic fact is that talking openly with a skilled, caring listener
about their *reasons* for dying lessens that terrible possibility. (See
"Communication/Empathy," Part 9.) So suicide talk is both the
fire *alarm* and *extinguisher.*

A second source of parental blindness is thinking that teens
think like us. A suicidal impulse to an adult can be whisked away
quickly and safely with thoughts borne by experience and brain
maturity: "I've been knocked down before and the sun always
rose in the morning." Your kid might have neither the experience
nor the brain wiring to understand that the sun will show up.
(See "Adolescent Brain Development," Part 9.)

The How

If you've allotted yourself one moment in your parenting life to
keep cool under intense fire, use that moment now, because a

suicidal kid who shuts up to avoid upsetting his parents is much more likely to die. I've read too many teen suicide notes portraying the ultimate irony of kids ending their lives *so as not to burden their families anymore*. Think about that horror for a moment, and then calm yourself so thoroughly that your kid senses that he can tell you horrifying thoughts without your getting angry, dismissing him, giving him dumb advice, or going to pieces. His emotional vomiting works the same way as with food poisoning: it helps him spew out those terrible "toxins" so that they do less damage. In this way, your loving and calm demeanor means everything to your child's survival. He will use it to steady himself, to disarm his killer urges, and to remember that he is loved and supported by wise people who know all about cold, dark nights and warm, bright sunrises.

WANT TO LEARN MORE?

The Power to Prevent Suicide: A Guide for Teens Helping Teens, by Richard E. Nelson, Judith C. Galas, and Pamela Espeland (Free Spirit Publishing, 2006)

PART 7

SEX AND DATING ISSUES

Don't worry mom... You don't need to give me "The Talk"...
I already asked Google.

IF YOU ARE reading this, you must have just discovered that your child is now a sexual creature. Welcome to your nightmare.

I understand. You always knew that your girl or boy would also be a woman or man one day, but . . . really, you didn't. You always harbored this secret, bizarre belief that your child would not be as sexually driven as you were as a teen, that somehow your kid would rise above all that stuff until at least age, I don't know, twenty-five or thirty? And you were comforted by knowing that, with a little luck, you might be dead by then anyway. So no worries. Am I right?

Your own level of denial might not be as radical as my own, but all of us deny our kids' sexuality to some extent, which is exactly the one thing we cannot do. For the truly frightening reality is that as sexually preoccupied as we were as adolescents, our teens are much worse. Not because they're worse people, but because they're in a worse culture, one that is obsessed with sexual behavior. (See "Identity" and "Sexuality" in Part 9.) They have been pounded with sexual training from the day they first stared at a TV set, with the girls in particular being powerfully programmed to believe that their primary worth and function on this planet is sexual.

What's that you said? All is cool 'cause there's sex ed at school? *No, there isn't!* Sure, they get the form and function stuff there, but that's not nearly enough. What the schools cannot (and should not) provide is the truly sexy parts of sex, namely the values, the codes, and the moral identity aspects. That *must* remain the purview of the parent.

"OK, Dr. Bradley," you sigh. "*You* try having the sex talk with my kid. He puts his hands over his ears and sings the Kreplachian national anthem until I stop." Of course he does. You see, "the sex talk" should actually be ten thousand mini-talks that begin at birth and continue forever, not one five-hour marathon in the study. The topic should become normalized, one frequently referenced for years in small snippets of thirty-second chats. (See "Communication/Empathy," Part 9.) These should be prompted by screen images: "This movie shows that prostitute as cool and having a good time. Do you think that's the way it really is for those people?" Or song lyrics: "This artist wants to be a pimp? What do you think about that?" Or news articles: "That paper says that rape is a sex crime. Do you think rape is about sex or about violence?"

And much (or most) of the talk should be silent, as in allowing our kids to see our own sexual values in action. By the way, what exactly do we display to our children? Do we treat people with sexual dignity, or do we leer and make provocative jokes? Do we respect our partners, or do we like to flirt? Are we faithful? Do we dress appropriately, or do we go way out of our way to draw sexual attention? Think hard about these things, because in the minds of our children, our actions will outshout our words every time.

If you've been doing none of this right (as is true for too many of us), is it too late? Not at all, so get a grip. In fact, it's even more effective to start this approach while you're dealing with one of the following scenarios, since now the topic is so very real to your child. Remember, sex and dating are rarely fatal diseases and most often become dangerous only when they're ignored. You managed to survive, and so will your kid.

Dates a Jerk

"Johnny loves me sooo much that he gets crazy jealous if I see my friends."

—MAGGIE, AGE SIXTEEN

The What

DO

- Know that now is the time for cool and disciplined diplomacy, not angry mandates.
- Know love forbidden by a parent becomes love irresistible to a teen.
- Know that you're likely seeing only a small part of the craziness.
- Know that boys *and girls* can be controlling and abusive.

- Watch for signs of physical abuse with girls *and boys* (bruises, welts, injury-concealing clothing/makeup, wearing huge sunglasses all the time).
- Watch for signs of emotional abuse with girls *and boys* (withdrawal from friends, activities, family time; poor hygiene; changes in appetite/sleep).
- Calmly raise your concerns to your child.
- Impose safety limits without telling your teen whom to love.
- Invite the jerk into your house at every opportunity. (Keep your friends close and your enemies closer.)
- Allow your kid to learn safely about bad relationships. (A thing better learned at sixteen than thirty-six.)
- Forbid contact if your teen admits to being physically abused, and call the police.
- Immediately get your child to a counselor if you see possible evidence of abuse or crippling control that she denies. (See "Getting Help," Part 9.)

DON'T

- Outright forbid the relationship (unless there are physical risks).
- Underestimate the power of teen love or the deficits of teen brains. (See "Adolescent Brain Development," Part 9.)
- Do nothing; your kid will assume that this crazy behavior is normal.
- Criticize or demean the jerk to your child (unless you want a new in-law).

The Why

Incredibly, about one-third of our daughters find themselves trapped in an abusive/controlling relationship before they escape high school. But the antidote to that epidemic seems counterintuitive to us parents. For example, do you know how to magically transform a dislikable, abusive creep into Brad Pitt or Angelina Jolie? *Forbid your teen to see the creep.* That's a surefire way to turn what might have been a bizarre but passing fancy into an unending Romeo-and-Juliet passion play. Do what you must to keep your kid safe but *learning*. (See "Parenting Teenagers," Part 9.) If you just forbid all contact, the relationship learning always ends and the running sometimes begins (as in fleeing to the other coast and getting pregnant in the bargain). That relationship learning is critical to helping your kid avoid her next controlling jerk when the eventual stakes might include a ten-year marriage and two babies.

The How

Impose safety restrictions as you must, but don't stop the relationship (unless there is physical abuse) or disrespect the jerk to your child. ("Honey, I worry that things are not so good in your relationship. Whom you date is your business, but your safety is mine, so I'll ask you to see him only here or when you're with a group of friends. He's welcome in our home anytime you like.") Keep Mr./Ms. Wrong in the unforgiving light of day, sitting nastily at your Sunday dinner table next to good adult role models for a "compare and contrast" exercise for your teen. The jerk's angry behaviors will stick out like a sore thumb for your child to ponder. Then sit back and wait. I happen to know (professionally and personally) only too well that that's easier said than done, but I also know that time then works to your advantage. Brad Pitt/Angelina Jolie will lose the super-attractive quality of being hated by parents, and his/her imperfections will become impossible to overlook. Offer an ear when you see a tear, but don't press too hard for information. And if your child tells you a story that makes you want to punch out the jerk, just listen quietly and ask what your teen thinks/feels. Punching out (or even insulting) the jerk will stop the learning. Let your kid work this out so that the lesson lasts a lifetime.

WANT TO LEARN MORE?

But I Love Him: Protecting Your Teen Daughter from Controlling, Abusive Dating Relationships, by Jill Murray (Harper Paperbacks, 2001)

Homosexual, Might Be

"I'd rather be black than gay; because when you're black you don't have to tell your mother."

—CHARLES PIERCE

In this section the term *gay* describes any sexual orientation other than heterosexual.

The What

DO

- Know that in your teenager's world the worst (and most used) put-down word is *gay*.
- Know that science is pretty sure that sexual orientation is an unchangeable biological difference, not a "lifestyle choice."
- Know that the odds are that your kid doesn't want to be gay and so might hate himself for being *who he cannot help being*. (That's called a rock and a hard place.)
- Know that teen sexual identity is a fluid thing for a while, and those feelings may change. (See "Sexuality," Part 9.)
- Know that gay teens have a terrible time telling their parents, especially their fathers.

- Know that sexual orientation crises play a role in *many* teen suicides.
- Tell your kid that his sexual identity can never change your parental love for him.
- Suggest that your child chat with a helper. (See "Getting Help," Part 9.)

DON'T

- React with anger, fear, or dismay. If you truly love your child, you'll put your own biases aside.
- Push your kid to acknowledge a sexual identity (even if you are fairly sure it's not heterosexual).
- Share what he tells you with anyone else without his permission.
- Tell your teen that he is or is not gay, even if he seems conflicted and confused.
- Attempt to change your teen's orientation with therapy. Objective research says that "reorientation" is not possible. (Although damage from that "therapy" is very possible.)

The Why

Adolescent sexual development has become a battleground of powerful political, religious, and cultural forces, all converging to create a lot of terrible pain for a lot of wonderful kids who were dealt the biological cards of sexual differences. This takes a tough process and makes it near impossible. First, gay teens must contend with a complex psychological turmoil within them as they try to reconcile with their sexuality. Second, they must navigate a culture that demands that they "make a sexual choice." And that "choice" (one about as voluntary as eye color) can literally destroy their friendships, their family, their education, their future . . . pretty much their entire world can go up in smoke with one quiet declaration: "I think I'm gay." Don't believe the hype that your teen's culture is now accepting of such differences. It generally is not. Teens (particularly the males) are *just not allowed* to be sexually different. (It can be a capital offense in some places.)

Your son will be using your initial reaction to his confiding in you as a test to see if he can be who he is and still be loved. Your behavior may well set the course for the rest of his life. It might even save that life. Think very hard. This is parent "game time."

The How

First, do whatever it takes to get your own emotions in hand, *regardless* of what they are. I know this sounds impossible, but this is still your child, and you are still the parent. Next, listen to your teen better than you ever have. He's likely terribly confused and/or conflicted and desperately needing a lovingly quiet sounding board on which he can sort all of this stuff out. He may not even be sure about any of this, but don't push his process one way or another or you might distort it in ways that can cause great damage. This is a developmental issue that must proceed on its own timeline. You cannot talk him in or out of an orientation, so just let him talk in whatever way he chooses without letting him perceive any differences in your feelings for him. Remember that he's likely feeling about as lonely and scared as he ever will in his life and thinks that if you are not in his corner, then he is truly alone. For a kid with sexual differences, that's a desperate and dangerous place to be. Your job is to show your child that while jerks may want to hate and fear him, good people will love and respect him for who he is, knowing that his sexuality is his *characteristic*, not his *character*. And that his orientation is about the *wiring within his brain* and not the *values within his heart*.

Tell him those things when he's finished talking, but show him those things *right now* by listening well. He will never need your love more.

WANT TO LEARN MORE?

Always My Child: A Parent's Guide to Understanding Your Gay, Lesbian, Bisexual, Transgendered or Questioning Son or Daughter, by Kevin Jennings and Pat Shapiro (Fireside, 2003)

Pornography, Watches

"Dad, I already know all about sex. I've got a computer."

The What

DO

- Calm down. He's not a pervert, he's a teen, and porn is a powerful tsunami flooding his world.
- Know that much of today's pornography is yesterday's sexual disorder (bestiality, torture, misogyny, and other bizarreness for which we have no labels).
- Know that the *average* age of first exposure to porn is *ten.*
- Know that exposure to pornography powerfully impacts teen sexual expectations, attitudes, values, and behaviors.
- Know that your Net porn filter works about as well as his "six-pack-abs-in-one-week" chair.
- *Calmly engage* this enemy with your kid: do some joint research into the "real deal" of porn to shape your teen's beliefs. (See "The How," following.)

- Get to a helper if your teen seems unable to curtail that "entertainment" since it can be addicting. (See "Getting Help," Part 9.)

DON'T

- Just snap out and punish him. (He'll just angrily go underground with this.)
- Think that you can keep this junk from getting to your child.
- Think that it won't impact your kid's beliefs about sex.
- Think that what your teen is watching is "just sex."

The Why

Your knee-jerk response to a porn threat to your child is likely the same as mine: to get better software. Unfortunately our mission is much more complex than downloading filters, and our battlefield is not only on our kids' computers but in their heads. Porn is so pervasive in your teenager's world that you cannot isolate him from the exposure: the best you can do is to *inoculate* him against the effects by helping him see porn for what it truly is. So use his porn offense not as a reason to punish but as an excuse to teach: "Son, your behavior shows us that it's time for you and me to research this subject together and see what we can learn about what porn really is about." (See "Parenting Teenagers," Part 9.)

If you just punish or police, you'll get an effect that might last a week. If you shape his *beliefs* about porn, you might protect him for a lifetime.

The How

Your goal is to take the "romance" out of porn (How's that for an oxymoron?) because it's typically presented in exciting, sanitized productions where the real human costs are neatly airbrushed out. Your method is to go behind the scenes to show the brutal realities so that the next time pornography beckons on his screen those cold-reality images pop into his head to compete with the erotic fantasy images on his screen. Do this by together researching the frightening effects of porn in this culture and then discussing what you find. Do a Net search of "impact of pornography," read the research together, and then take him out for a coffee for the discussion part. Ask questions such as "Do you think that porn hurts anyone?" and "Are men and women portrayed differently?" and "Is porn more a guy thing or a girl thing?" *Don't lecture, argue his answers, or preach.* The stories and facts you'll find on the Net will be powerful enough. Do make your own values very clear, but calmly present those in a positive light: "To me, son, porn takes something very beautiful and twists it into something very dirty." If you really want to pound home a point (and you've got the stomach), watch that porn segment he was watching with him. When he protests, ask him why he's so upset with your presence if this stuff is really OK.

Put your energies into helping your teen develop his own values and identity instead of just trying to control his behavior. If you don't, his culture will write those values for him, and that's another thing you don't want. Remember that parenting should be a game you play smart to win the season and not just a particular inning.

WANT TO LEARN MORE?

Pornified: How Pornography Is Transforming Our Lives, Our Relationships, and Our Families, by Pamela Paul (Times Books, 2005)

Sex, Is Having

"Mom, are you really sure you want me to tell you if I'm having sex?"

—JENNA, AGE THIRTEEN

The What

DO

- Stay cool. Your calm composure and wise words can be lifesaving.
- Know that the pressures on kids to be sexual have never been higher.
- Know that the mythology of "casual/harmless sex" is rampant among supposedly smart teens.
- Know that sexually transmitted diseases (STDs) and pregnancies have recently spiked among adolescents.
- Know that *the girls* are often the sexual aggressors in middle school and yet have mixed feelings or regrets about having sex. (See "Sexuality," Part 9.)
- Call for a "team meeting" that includes your kid's lover's parents. (Share this page with them.)
- Ask what the kids' plans are for the very possible pregnancy and how that would change their lives. When they answer that they're using protection . . .
- Punch up the safety rates for *teen* birth control and the failure rates for teen-parented families (about 90 percent and 100 percent, respectively).
- Eliminate the teen's rendezvous opportunities if she seems determined to continue, but as a last resort.
- See a helper ASAP. (See "Getting Help," Part 9.)

- Go crazy. Your screaming and yelling can be life destroying and life creating (as in "encouraging" a rebellion pregnancy).
- Think that teens are old enough for this. (They just look that way.)
- Play the morality/values cards first. (Those talks can come later.)
- Totally forbid the teen's relationship, unless you want to give her a great reason to run off with him. (See "Dates a Jerk," earlier in Part 7.)
- Cave in and allow the sex to continue. Lives are literally at stake.

The Why

First, focus on what *not* to do. Teens in love (or lust) can't respond well to religious/morality lectures, at least not quickly enough for this crisis, so *teach*, don't *preach*). For example, screaming at your daughter not to have sex can make that very act even more attractive. And forbidding her relationship can fan the small flames of desire into a firestorm of pregnancy risk and encourage her to run away to Mexico on a "romantic" Romeo-and-Juliet, misunderstood-teens adventure. But cold STD and pregnancy statistics can chill passion pretty effectively for antiabortion girls (who get to raise the kid for the rest of their lives) and for money-wise boys (who get to pay for the kid for the rest of their lives). And abortion or adoption can be very traumatic as well, facts that they've likely witnessed with their peers. They've heard all about these sex risks, but all of that information they got in school has been neatly packed away in a distant region of their brains for the duration of the romance. So you've got to dispassionately rain on their passion parade with risk data they've already heard but that will sound very different now that they're staring down the barrel of a possibly positive pregnancy or STD test.

The How

Restrict your teen's freedom as you must for safety, but do this only as a *last* resort since that will control her behavior for only a few weeks, instead of shaping her beliefs forever. And indefinite "lockdown" restrictions might push her even farther down that risk path. (See "Parenting Teenagers," Part 9.) Unfortunately for parents, teaching kids works best with calm conversation exactly at the time when you want to yell the most. So go *yell* at your kick-boxing partner while you're crazy and *talk* with your kid when you're calm. (See "Communication/Empathy," Part 9.) If you can strike that magic balance of safety and autonomy ("He's welcome here anytime, and you can hang out in groups with him, but visiting his house is out of the question for now."), time will provide your eventual antidote, since most teen romances have the shelf life of 2 percent milk.

As scary as this nightmare is for you, understand that your kid's "fruitless" sexual activity (no pregnancy) is your very much unwanted gift. For now you have a shot at the most powerful type of teaching that teens can experience, which is teaching while the lesson is *relevant* to their lives. Your lesson plan must be to shape her belief system about the relative gain/risk of sexual activity so that next time she might think twice—so that it's about not just her present "once-in-a-lifetime, forever-love soul mate" but the ten others she's going to meet in the next ten years.

WANT TO LEARN MORE?

The Underground Guide to Teenage Sexuality, by Michael J. Basso (Fairview Press, 2003)

Unhooked: How Young Women Pursue Sex, Delay Love and Lose at Both, by Laura Sessions Stepp (Riverhead Trade, 2008)

PART 8

SOCIAL ISSUES

Isn't it amazing? There you were thinking that your teenager was doing most of her learning on weekdays from 8:00 A.M. to 3:00 P.M., and suddenly it hit you that she is enrolled in *two* schools, not one. There's the important one you already knew about, the one with the smelly gym, scary bathrooms, and bad food. And then there's the *really* important one that you just began to notice: her "social school." That enrollment caught you by surprise, didn't it?

That's because we parents tend to toss our adolescents' relationship issues into that same low-priority basket that holds their choices of toothpaste, music, and movie interests. After all, how important can peers be to a mere kid? Answer: *even more important to him than yours are to you.*

Much like an ocean reef, a teenager's social network provides a vast diversity of interaction, an incredibly rich source of learning and growth. (See "Adolescent Psychological Development" and "Identity," Part 9.) This "social school" is a living learning laboratory where your teen gets to observe and test concepts that are much more important than anything he'll ever see in chemistry class. In "social school" your kid will learn about loyalty, respect, values, trust, character, compassion, negotiation, selflessness, codes of behavior, love, and a few other trivial things.

This is one of those examples of how your kid is in a very different place from you. When it comes to social issues, your schooling is mostly over. You largely know who you are, what you believe, and what things hold value for you. Because of that knowing, you have lots of supports that help you be affected less by negative social events such as fighting with a friend, being excluded from a group, or being hassled by a jerk. If things go badly at the golf course, you've still got your partner, work friends, neighbors, self-confidence, resilience, and so on. Your kid has few of those anchors and thus gets tossed around a lot harder by the storms of social crisis. The irony is that instead of avoiding those squalls, he needs to sail head-on through them to learn to eventually be more secure. Isn't that how you learned?

Yet hidden in that reef there are also sharp teeth and dangerous coral that can puncture a teen's fragile self-worth in a New York minute, and even put her at risk of physical harm. If something is important, she'll see it in social school. If it's scary, she'll see it there as well. So how do we parents protect our novice sailors and yet allow them to learn?

The fact is that the more we big fish (parents) interfere with life on that reef, the less the little fish learn. So if you decide to intervene in your kid's relationships, do so knowing that all learning will likely end and that your child may need to complete the lesson later on in life when the learning process can be much more costly. When it comes to social issues, "Let it be" should be our parental theme song, although that's admittedly a tune that sounds great until we start to see sharp teeth coming toward our kid. "Uh-oh" moments like those are when we earn those big bucks that parents get paid to decide if and when and how to intervene. The sections that follow will help you do just that.

What are the general guidelines? Mostly to do less, not more. Provide an empathic ear and not an expert's mouth. (See "Communication/Empathy," Part 9.) Remember that trial and error is usually the most effective kind of learning (as long as the learner survives to use the knowledge). Ask soft questions and offer quiet observations instead of taking hard control of your kid's social life: "Honey, I worry that things are not too cool at Susan's house. What do you think?"

Finally, when you are about to belly-flop onto that reef not so much to protect your kid but really to help *you* feel better, consider my wife's words of wisdom in reminding me that we want our kids to be learning these tough lessons while they are still in our home. When she sings "Let it Be," she adds the phrase "better at fourteen than at forty."

Bullied, Is Being

"Dad, I've discovered that the bigger they are, the harder they . . . hit!"

—BEN, AGE THIRTEEN

The What

DO

- Know that bullying can be physical, verbal, cyber, and silent (shunning).
- Know that the verbal/cyber/silent bullying can hurt more than the hitting.

- Know that what adults call harassment and assault kids are told is "teasing," "normal," "inevitable," and "toughening."
- Know that bullying wounds are linked with depression, shyness, truancy, and suicide.
- Know that, contrary to the myth, bullies are usually popular with their peers and with themselves (have good self-esteem).
- Know that bullies are usually bigger, more well liked, and stronger than their victims. (So fistfight solutions are movie myths.)
- Know that your teen might be too ashamed to tell you what's been happening.
- Know that bullying is best stopped by *long-term, ongoing, schoolwide programs*, not by individual bully/victim confrontations or mediations.
- Know that each victim must find *his own way* to cope and respond.
- Offer your loving ear, not your distancing advice. (See "Communication/Empathy," Part 9.)
- Offer to call the school. (Insist on this if the bullying is extreme.) But . . .
- Know that calling the school might make things worse if the staff are not well trained in bullying intervention.
- Know that bullying peaks in middle school and then slowly ebbs with each passing year.
- Ask if your kid ever thinks about hurting himself or about violent revenge plans. If he says yes, secure any weapons and see a helper immediately to evaluate those potentials. (See "Getting Help," Part 9.)

DON'T

- Think that fighting is the answer for your kid, *especially* if it was for you.
- Think that you know what your teen's response should be.

- Minimize this torture as "normal."
- Let your own anger or disappointment (because he won't fight?) keep him from sharing his.
- Call the school without the teen's permission, at least initially. (Schools sometimes make things worse.)
- Forget that the teen needs your love and support, not your hand-to-hand instruction.

The Why

Forget baseball. The national pastime for children is bullying, with over half having been targeted at one time or another. It's so common that we adults (who'd file charges if we were treated the same as our kids) don't really see it anymore. In fact, we often romanticize it as a normal and strengthening process, one that "builds character" like boot camp. But these victims are children, not soldiers, and they're "draftees," not volunteers. They're trapped in their schools and neighborhoods with jerks for whom we adults would get restraining orders.

The damage from bullying is so great that you must do something—but what? With apologies to Hollywood, fighting very rarely works and usually makes things worse. (Win or lose, the social ostracism usually just increases.) If you're intending to get your school to do something, you'd better first see what that something might be. If administrators talk about schoolwide training programs, push for that. (These are dramatically effective.) If they talk about chastising the bully or forcing mediation, let your kid make that call. (The outcomes of these options are often lousy.) Bullying is more a social/community/group process than a disagreement between two competitors, so the only real solution is in changing how bullying is seen in that *community*. Without that community focus, there is probably not much good that the school will do for your suffering child.

The How

But there is a lot that you can do on your own, a system I call "Outlast the Bastards." First, give your kid your caring ear, that most healing and least used of all parent tools. Listening well is perhaps 50 percent of the cure. Next, point out to the teen that this insanity peaks in middle school, decreases through high school, and virtually disappears in college. Telling your child that, in college, *bullies* are the ones who get laughed at and shunned gives him hope that life gets better (which it most definitely does). Then ask if he'd like your help in developing some strategies to survive until then. Brainstorm to make a list of all options from which he can pick and choose. Start by suggesting thermonuclear devices and work downward from there. (Humor helps a lot.) Have him evaluate strategies such as ignoring (easier said than done), avoiding, soft retorting (as in shrugs and "whatever"), traveling with friends, making new friends through activities, and so on. That lengthy list—even if some of the strategies aren't practical—will help him feel a bit of control just when he desperately needs some. If he's too reactive to the taunting, use Fred Hanna's "Freedom Challenge." (See the "Want to Learn More?" list that follows.) Point out that when you react to bullies, *they own you.* Reframe the act of maintaining his composure and walking away not as cowardice but as a victory for freedom since the jerk no longer controls your kid's reactions. That's a very tough thing to do, but it might be his least painful option.

Repeat the preceding drill periodically to adapt to the changes in your teen's growing maturity and in the nature of the bullying. Most of all, keep a sharp eye and a caring ear out for the terrible depression that can result from bullying. Then hunker down to "Outlast the Bastards." Speaking as a veteran "bastard outlaster," I can personally attest that living well is indeed the best revenge.

WANT TO LEARN MORE?

The Bully, the Bullied, and the Bystander: From Preschool to High School—How Parents and Teachers Can Help Break the Cycle of Violence, by Barbara Coloroso (Collins, 2004)

Please Stop Laughing at Us: One Survivor's Extraordinary Quest to Prevent School Bullying, by Jodee Blanco (Benbella Books, 2008)

Therapy with Difficult Clients, by Fred Hanna (American Psychological Association, 2003)

Clique, Is Excluded by A

"They couldn't say what exactly is wrong with me. They just say that *everything* is."

—ALEXA, AGE THIRTEEN

The What

DO

- Know that roughly half of teens belong to cliques (groups of three to ten very similar, "popular" kids).
- Know that to your kid *popular* really means "powerful and dominant," not necessarily well liked or nice.
- Know that cliques are power-oriented structures designed primarily to control other kids, not to make good friends.
- Know that clique membership to your child might equal a great job in a powerful corporation to you.
- Know that cliques offer wonderful security to the high-status members ("queens/kings") and terrible stress for the low-status members.

- Ask her to define the exact loss *and gain* that comes with being *rejected* by a clique (loss of status, gain of independence, and so on).
- Ask her to define the exact loss *and gain* that comes from being *accepted* by a clique (gain of status, loss of independence, being required to abandon "loser" friends, and so on).
- Ask your teen to name the people she *admires, likes, and enjoys* (not *envies*) the most, and then ask whether they are "clique queens" or not (although they might be clique members).
- Ask what it is that she admires, likes, and enjoys about those kids.
- Ask whether your teen would rather be the well-liked kid or the clique queen/king.
- See a helper if she's really suffering from her exclusion. (See "Getting Help," Part 9.)

DON'T

- Argue with your teen's answers or tell her that cliques are stupid (they're not to her).
- Be dismissive or underestimate how devastating clique rejection might be. (Some kids become terribly depressed.)
- Demean the queens. They might still be your kid's idols even after having been so cruel. (This is not about nice; it's about power.)

The Why

Here is another of those parenting tasks where you need to focus on the long-term goals (your child's identity/values development) in addition to the short-term crisis ("I'll never be popular"); see "Identity," Part 9. Her rejection pain provides a powerful energy for her to learn about social relationships, what they're about, and what types she really wants in her own life. Thinking this through carefully will help her define what things she truly values in others and then set about building on those kinds of friendships that will offer her so much more than any clique.

The How

When it comes to teaching kids, asking them questions works so much better than telling them what to do. (See "Decision Making" and "Parenting Teenagers" in Part 9.) Use the questions just noted to help your teen move through the longer-term identity issues about the nature of friendship, but also pay lots of attention to her short-term pain. Her rejection from a "silly" clique can be as devastating to her as a job rejection from a dominant company might be to you. Offer lots of hugs and quiet listening before you use those questions to help your kid with both her present pain and her future friendship choices. Help her see that popular cliques can seem like all that matters in the world, all that matters, that is, until we lose a close friendship. Help her to eventually learn that the subtle gold of one true friend outshines the glitter and glamour of a hundred "popular" ones.

WANT TO LEARN MORE?

Mean Chicks, Cliques, and Dirty Tricks: A Real Girl's Guide to Getting Through the Day with Smarts and Style, by Erika V. Shearin Karres (Adams Media Corporation, 2004)

Friends, Has No

"I guess my invitation got lost in the mail."

The What

DO

- Know that friendless teens are at risk for poor self-esteem, delinquency, drug abuse, depression, and troubled relationships as adults.

- Know that being isolated makes friendships harder, which makes kids "weirder," which makes friendships harder, which . . . it's a vicious cycle.
- Know that even talking about this can be agonizing for your child (from shame, guilt, and embarrassment), so be gentle and take this in small doses.
- Tell him that making and maintaining friendships requires certain *assets*, *skills*, and *practice* (much like tennis).
- Push to see a helper since this is a *very critical* issue. (See "Getting Help," Part 9.)
- Have that helper also check for other possible friendship-failing factors (social anxiety, depression, social skills disorders).
- Tell him that the older he gets, the easier "tennis" (friendship) will get since older kids are much nicer and more accepting of differences.

DON'T

- Underestimate how devastating this can be for your kid. That loneliness can be profoundly painful.
- Become too emotional or reactive. Put friendship problems in the context of being lousy at some sport (a temporary lack of *skill*, not a permanent lack of *character*).
- Just ignore this. The stakes for friendless kids are high.
- Quit selling at your teen's first refusal to try to change things by seeing a helper. Calmly revisit this periodically until he agrees to take a shot.

The Why

There's little more hurtful to a parental heart than watching your teen navigate adolescence without friends. That pain is felt ten times over by your child, a pain that reflects Mother Nature's denied demand for your kid to be social. This is a critical piece of your teen's development, one that impacts things such as identity, mental health, adult relationship skills, achievement, self-esteem, happiness, resilience . . . that list goes on and on. Their possible statements to the contrary, teens do not want to be isolated from their peers. Know that if yours rants continually about all kids being "stupid, immature, and conformist sellouts with whom I wouldn't be caught dead," he's really just defending himself against the terrible loneliness and confusion of social rejection. There are indeed lids for every pot, and your job is to help your child find and connect with kids similar to him.

The How

Assume your teen wants and needs friends, and then gently talk about this. Give his pain lots of space in your chats by quietly listening to his rants and/or sobs (see "Communication/Empathy," Part 9), but when he's done ask if he's willing to try to improve things. Know that the pain of rejection can be so scary that he might rather stay alone than risk another round of hurt, at least at first consideration. So take this slowly in several small conversations, asking him to think (and/or journal) about this. Use that tennis metaphor. Tell him that some kids are naturals at "tennis" while others need *asset* training, *skill* coaching, and a willingness to *practice*. Point out that being bad at "tennis" is nothing to be ashamed of and that friend making is a sport that *can be learned if he wants*. Next, review the list of teen friendship *assets* with your kid that he might want to build. Those include (1) *conformity* (acting/appearing similar to other kids), (2) *involvement* (in clubs and activities), (3) *achievement* (grades, community service, sports), and (4) *physical attractiveness* (appearance, hygiene, smile, easy manner—*not thinness or buffness*).

State that your child's friendship *skills* (engagement, conversation, flexibility, connection strengthening) can grow with some professional "coaching" from a counselor and a willingness to practice from him. (See "Getting Help," Part 9.)When he's ready, see a helper and also set up a meeting with his school counselor, who likely will have a hundred helpful options right there in the building. (School is a built-in friend factory with a hundred different socializing clubs and activities.)

Those strategies (i.e., activities) might take some time to bear friendship fruit, so be sure to get your child into some immediate success experiences to help him with his hurting self-esteem. Those might include hanging out with supportive adults, taking skills classes, caretaking younger and/or special-needs kids, or volunteering at the retirement home. His peer aloneness is a tough enough cross to bear. Don't allow your child's lousy skills at "tennis" grow into a terrible loneliness that can bring him to doubt his very worth.

WANT TO LEARN MORE?

The Friendship Factor: Helping Our Children Navigate Their Social World and Why It Matters for Their Success and Happiness, by Kenneth Rubin and Andrea Thompson (Viking Adult, 2002)

Peer Pressure, Is Influenced By

"But everybody does it!"

The What

DO

- Know that peer pressure is a powerful influence, especially on younger teens.

- Know that kids typically choose peers who are *already* similar to themselves, for better and for worse.
- Know that most pressure from peers is *positive* (such as to finish school) and that most kids are most influenced by *positive pressures* from peers, not negative.
- Know that most kids don't directly push others to do bad things, but *their* modeling and her need for acceptance can influence your child.
- Know that unconfident kids are the most easily influenced. (See "Identity," Part 9.)
- Know that even positive peers can take your child too far away from you. (So compete for some of her time.)
- Go all-out to keep your kid's friends as close as possible (pizza parties, movies, sleepovers, and so on). Make your house *their* house. And when teens refuse free food and lodging, watch out.

DON'T

- Disrespect or disparage your teenager's friends. You'll only make them her "band of sisters."
- Judge books by covers. Some of the best-looking kids have the worst values; some of the worst-looking kids have the best.
- Forbid her friendships without good cause. That can become good motivation to find bad friends.
- Blame your kid's bad behaviors solely on her peers. Those kids are most likely only a reflection of her own preexisting problems.
- Take her rejections personally. ("Mom, I'm too old to be hanging out with you. And, besides, the kids are waiting for me, OK?")
- Quit competing for your teen's time. ("Well, do two tickets to Ozzfest interest you?")

The Why

Peers are not the source of all evil that many of us parents believe them to be. Research has shown that most of our kids' peers have a *positive* effect on them. Much of our suspicious reaction to the peers is due to our jealousy and sadness as we watch our previously devoted child start to ditch us for her friends. It's tough suddenly not being cool in the eyes of our kid, but that's nature's way. Peers are supposed to have substantial impact on your teen to help her grow, experiment, and figure out who the heck she is to help her develop her identity. But much of this parental loss is temporary since peer power peaks in middle school and then slowly ebbs back in favor of the parents. So during that "away" phase, just keep an eye on how your kid's peers might be impacting her. If they change her hair, music, or politics, that's actually good, and you should respect and honor her differences. That's how she learns about the world and her place in it. If they change her drug/alcohol/school/violence attitudes in the wrong direction, that's bad, and you need to skillfully challenge those differences. Whether her peers are good or bad, during her "away tour," be sure to keep your kid connected with you to some degree since she can become completely consumed by those peers, good or bad.

The How

Your plan should start with the least intrusive interventions and slowly ratchet up the control level as you need. The idea is to maximize her learning (by allowing lots of exploration room) and minimize her danger (from drugs/sex/violence). View this as a continuum of control. If her decisions remain good, impose as little control as possible. As your concerns increase, slowly start to interject soft questions and statements for her to ponder: "Honey, it's your job to choose your friends, but it's my job to worry. Some of those kids might be bad news. Please be careful." As her decisions and behavior deteriorate, start to slowly restrict her access to those peers, but make it clear that this is not about controlling her choices of friends but about questioning her choices of *behaviors*: "After that prank incident I'm afraid that you can't hang out unsupervised with them for a while, but they're welcome here anytime."

Erect firm fences if your teen's behaviors cross into serious issues: "Since we know that they do drugs, I'm afraid that you need to step back from that group. I love you too much to risk your going down that path. How can I help you make new friends?"

Always show your child that with increased behavioral responsibility will come increased social autonomy. At the same time, work hard to increase the attractiveness of her spending more time with her "old" family. (You know, the one into which she was born.) Offer to let her choose activities for the family to do, and support those choices no matter how painful they might be. (Did I mention that my wife actually went to Ozzfest with my son?) Beg, borrow, and bribe to get as much time as you can to compete with those peer influences, especially if you see them as negative. But throughout all this, be sure to keep your cool. For when it comes to disagreements about teen friends, your yelling and excessive control can make martyrs out of molehills.

WANT TO LEARN MORE?

The Courage to Be Yourself: True Stories by Teens About Cliques, Conflicts, and Overcoming Peer Pressure, by Al Desetta (Free Spirit Publishing, 2005)

Peer Pressure: Deal with It Without Losing Your Cool, by Elaine Slavens (Lorimer, 2004)

Staying Connected to Your Teenager: How to Keep Them Talking to You and How to Hear What They're Really Saying, by Michael Riera (Perseus Publishing, 2003)

Shy, Is

"I'm not as good as other kids. I'm shy."

—GRANT, AGE THIRTEEN

Also see "Friends, Has No," earlier in Part 8.

The What

DO

- Know that shyness is not who your teen is but *how he feels.*
- Know that shy kids usually feel lousy about themselves.
- Know that shyness can be a biochemical disorder or a learned response (from being bullied or abused) or both, and it can damage your teen's development.
- Know that *50 percent* of adults report having struggled with it.
- Ask your kid if he's OK with being so shy, but go softly. (He might feel too ashamed to talk about it.)
- Work to help your child see shyness as his *limiting characteristic*, not as his *limited character.*
- Ask if he would like to do something to change.
- Tell your teen that many famous folks found successful careers in doing things to shake off their shyness. (See shake yourshyness.com.)
- Model your own antishyness techniques (greeting others warmly, asking others about themselves, forcing yourself to

social events you want to duck and then reporting to your kid how much fun you had even though you resisted going).

- Ask if he'd like to get some help to change. (See "Getting Help," Part 9.)

- Believe that your teen prefers living like this.
- Joke about or mock him about his shyness or allow others to do so.
- Nag, demand, or try to force him to change.
- Just ignore it and hope that it goes away.

The Why

Shyness is less a facet of personality and more a limiter of personality. It is not *who someone is* but rather a serious condition that prevents your kid from being who he is and from becoming who he wants to become. Left untreated, it may just go away on its own, but in the interim, its costs can be substantial. Shyness can rob your child of so much of his teen life that it can prevent him from achieving the number-one goal of adolescence: *figuring out who he is*. (See "Identity," Part 9.)

The How

Research the Web with your kid for the amazing stories of successful people who struggled (and who continue to struggle) with painful shyness. A very short list includes historical figures such as Albert Einstein, Theodore Roosevelt, Eleanor Roosevelt, Thomas Jefferson, and Ulysses S. Grant; entertainer/actors such as Brad Pitt, Julia Roberts, David Bowie, Michelle Pfeiffer, David Letterman, George Harrison, Gloria Estefan, Jim Carrey, Tom Hanks, and Kevin Costner; and athletes Mia Hamm and Cathy

Rigby. And those are just the ones secure enough to admit to their shyness. Then ask your child to let you know when he's ready to attack this problem with the aid of a helper. In the interim, take every opportunity to openly model the common three-step process of shyness that most people experience to a minor extent when faced with a new social setting: the irrational, anticipatory fear ("A silly part of me says that all of the other people will hate me"), the debate in your head ("The smarter part of me says that I'll probably have fun"), and the decision ("I'm so mad at myself for not going" or, hopefully, "I'm so glad that I went; I would have missed a great time").

Until your kid signals that he's ready, focus extra time and attention on helping him remember all that's good about him, such as his accomplishments and/or his compassion. Work with him to find activities where he can socialize in a less stressful way (team sports, community services, and so on).

Be sure to remind your teen of the powerful words uttered by a painfully shy person, someone who ended up accomplishing a fair amount in her life: "No one can make you feel inferior without your consent"—Eleanor Roosevelt.

WANT TO LEARN MORE?

The Shyness and Social Anxiety Workbook: Proven Techniques for Overcoming Your Fears, by Martin M. Antony and Richard P. Swinson (New Harbinger Publications, 2000)

Shyness: What It Is, What to Do About It, by Philip G. Zimbardo (Addison Wesley Publishing, 1990)

PART 9

THE TWENTY-MINUTE GUIDE TO THE NEW-MILLENNIUM TEEN

So...
She's been LOL-ing with her BFF's B/F and he has been ROFL with J-Fed's G\F and totally JK-ing with her peeps. I think...

Why you shouldn't snoop

WELCOME TO THE most arrogant section of a most arrogant book. Here's where we take bushels of information about parenting adolescents and sift out the key kernels you need to quickly understand your teens, their world, and how to effectively parent them. While the other book sections are very specific in scope, these topics are much broader and provide the background against which you should view any particular kid concern.

The arrogant part here is that there are many lengthy and excellent books dedicated exclusively to each one of these topics. (You'll find several recommended throughout this text.) One of my peers scanned this section, commented on its ambitious mission to do so much in so little time, and dubbed it "The Drive-By Guide to Parenting Adolescents." Cute.

Actually I wasn't terribly offended since that awful shooting metaphor almost fits in one sense. As parents of teenagers we are often operating out of a sense of urgency (if not panic) and in a mode where we just react to whatever comes at us. Perhaps that works in football, but it usually makes thing worse in parenting. The information you'll find under these topics will help you be proactive instead of reactive so you can quickly handle your immediate crisis but also, and even more important, skillfully avoid the next one.

Resolving your immediate concern can be handled by reading only the particular topic to which you were referred. Avoiding the next problem is best done by reading about all of these subjects as a kind of mini-handbook on teen parenting. I believe that if you read over this entire section you will own a decent set of tools that you can apply to a host of other challenges that your kid hasn't even dreamt of yet. But they're coming.

So if you want my opinion (speaking more as a parent than as a shrink), I'd read the whole section. I promise to keep it short and sweet—well, short anyway.

Adolescent Brain Development

Yes, they do have one. No, it's not the one you had hoped.

It has long been thought that, since six-year-old children and grown adults have similar-size brains, teenagers certainly must have adult brains. That belief is about as accurate as saying that a Ferrari and a Yugo have the same capabilities since they are both small cars. Ferrari (adult) brains have all sorts of amazing proficiencies that teen brains simply don't have—yet. While Yugos never grow up to drive like Ferraris, teens do grow the *wiring* for adult skills. But that's only the first step in acquiring those skills.

You see, in early adolescence the brain starts major neurological and hormonal renovations that set the stage for an amazing transformation from child thinking into adult thinking. This is a time when kids' brains are building sophisticated wiring, making them capable of seeing and understanding things that they simply could not comprehend before. This is the time when they can truly begin to define themselves as positive human beings in terms of their values, codes of conduct, philosophy, and beliefs. Or not. It all depends on the programming that is downloaded to the new wiring.

What gets programmed into that awakening brain depends primarily on the world surrounding that brain. And, believe it or not, the most powerful programmer of your kid's brain, dear parent, is you. The primary way those young brains learn is by observing and modeling the adults around them, most of all their parents. So, for better or for worse, our teenagers are very much a reflection of *who we adults are*, not what kind of adults we tell our children to become.

As a dispassionate shrink reading research, I see that as a reliable finding. As an imperfect parent looking in the mirror, I see that as a frightening worry. As both, I see Mother Nature's sense of humor in the fact that adolescents who do the best are usually the ones who have close relationships with their parents. The joke, of course, is that maintaining a great relationship with a teenager can sometimes get so hard that too many parents quit the game *without ever realizing they were winning even when they thought they were losing.*

They quit because those miraculous brain changes also present maddening relationship challenges that can turn family functions into frightening firefights that everyone avoids because they get tired of being shot at. Because of that rewiring, most adolescents will at times become a tad moody, disorganized, depressed, anxious, angry, aggressive, uncommunicative, and/or sleep deprived. And sometimes that's just on Monday. While most of those challenges usually just resolve on their own by seventeen or eighteen, trying to get close to a younger teenager can often feel like trying to hug an alligator.

But the teen brain renovation that most rudely confronts astonished parents concerns the prefrontal cortex. That's the part that helps us adults accurately predict outcomes of actions ("If I drive at 100 miles an hour, terrible things will happen"), rein in our dangerous impulses ("Punching that arrogant cop is a bad idea"), and regulate our behavior with a moral code ("I'd like to have sex with that woman, but I love my wife too much to do that"). Small things like that. Teens are only in the *process* of finalizing that key brain part. The outside of the "building" can look finished, but inside you find that it's not yet ready for occupancy.

So what to do? Pick your battles, avoid overreacting to the small stuff, and, beyond all else, stay close to your child, especially when he wants to be far from you. (See "Adolescent Psychological Development" and "Parenting Teenagers" later in Part 9.) Take it on faith that your teen *does* want to be close with you and knows that he still needs some supervision and structure but that it's just a lot harder for him to show that for now. Your child's brain will eventually wire in, and if you've kept both your cool and your closeness with your kid, you'll very likely be the parent of a young adult who holds values amazingly similar to your own. It turns out that *modeling* patience, tolerance, and love is a great way to win the hearts hiding inside bubbling teenage brains, even the ones that yell that you are dumber than snow.

WANT TO LEARN MORE?

The Primal Teen, by Barbara Strauch (Doubleday, 2003)
Why Do They Act That Way?, by David Walsh (Free Press,
    2005)
*Yes, Your Teen Is Crazy! Loving Your Kid Without Losing Your
    Mind*, by Michael J. Bradley (Harbor Press, 2003)

Adolescent Culture

Take a walk on the wild side.

When your child tells you that you don't understand what it's like to be a teenager, believe her—you don't. Yes, you were once an adolescent, but, you weren't a teen in her world, and that makes all the difference. Contemporary culture hammers kids twenty-four/seven with powerful suggestions to engage in risky sex, drugs, and violence to a degree far beyond that of any other generation of young folks. And it does this with the unprecedented power and efficiency of electronics.

These crazy suggestions (or "prompts") are images in movies and videos, lyrics in songs, chat room exchanges, plots in TV shows, "newscasts" about dysfunctional public figures, and so on. Researchers have lots of scary data showing that these prompts infiltrate suggestible adolescent brains (see "Adolescent Brain Development," earlier in Part 9) in ways that whisper, "Hey, kid! This stuff is cool, adult, and harmless. Everybody else is doing it, so why not you?"

Can these prompts really affect behavior? Increasingly the research says yes. For example, a recent study found that kids who see lots of on-screen cigarette smoking (in movies and videos) have exponentially higher risks of smoking than kids who see little. Other research has suggested that sexually explicit and misogynistic song lyrics may promote high-risk sexual activity in girls. "Advertising" does work, especially with impressionable adolescent brains. So much so that some professional associations that deal with children have begun to demand that the producers of these prompts stop sending these powerful messages to our children.

At least in part as a result of this propaganda, the rates of most risky teen behaviors have never been higher. While some surveys dispute these data, those numbers are mostly from self-report inventories where kids are asked to write down if they're participating in sex, drugs, and/or violence. Some research has found that today's technology/information-savvy teens are under-reporting these behaviors by as much as 30 to 40 percent since they no longer trust that any disclosures can be kept secret.

Regardless of whose numbers you trust, the culture is clearly causing disturbing behaviors with this generation of adolescents. In fact, the only risk numbers that are worse than the kids' are those of *their parents*. That's right. The adult sex, drugs, and violence risk behaviors in the parents of teens have never been higher either. And adolescents don't produce the music, create the movies, or market the porn. That's on us grown-ups. This scary teen culture is simply a reflection of our own adult culture. Our inability to control ourselves has us looking pretty nuts to the teens we love to criticize.

And there lies the cause and the cure for this cultural conundrum. When we surround kids with irresponsible and crazy adults, we usually get irresponsible and crazy kids. When we surround kids with responsible and safe adults, we tend to get more responsible and safer kids. (See "Parenting Teenagers.") When it comes to shaping children, the only thing that can overcome the raucous and stunning power of a crazy culture is the quiet and even more stunning power of a loving parent.

WANT TO LEARN MORE?

A Tribe Apart: A Journey into the Heart of American Adolescence, Patricia Hersch (Ballantine Books, 1999)

Adolescent Psychological Development

Nature's method to the madness

Perhaps the most calming words a perplexed parent can read are those describing how and why adolescents change. Mother Nature does indeed have a building plan in mind to transform your teen from a happy and helpless child into a happy and competent adult. But renovating a house or a human always involves some unhappy and chaotic times of conflict. Still, most veteran renovators of kitchens and kids agree that at the end of the struggle and conflict, the product is well worth the pain. In fact, it can be magnificent—if you handle things well. The first step is to understand the ingenious plan causing the chaos.

There are many models available for viewing child development, but psychologist Erik Erikson offered one that many parents find helpful. He believed that kids are prewired with renovation plans to develop four assets in childhood you could call *trust, autonomy, initiative,* and *industry,* qualities they build through testing, conflict, and ultimate resolution. Children begin building these qualities when they are young, and each one is critical to your teen's ability to perform her number one adolescent task: figuring out who the heck she is, or *developing her identity.* (See

"Identity.") While the bulk of these four tasks should be finished before adolescence starts, these struggles often reappear in adolescence in ways that can present challenges for parents. But if you can view these things as connected parts of a masterful plan, it becomes much easier to stay calm and to maintain a loving connection with your kid as she journeys through her adolescence.

Trust can appear when your young teen can suddenly seem lost to you, overwhelmingly controlled by his peers. Many kids (the boys in particular) disappear into their "caves" (rooms) for about a year, coming out mostly to feed, snarl at their biological families, and demand more time to spend with their new, "better" families: *their friends*. This is when many parents cry themselves to sleep at night, mourning the "loss" of their child to his peers.

They'd cry less if they knew that not only is this usually temporary, but it's also the time where their kids are unknowingly but intensively studying relationships between people (who are not family members) to learn about vital concepts such as trustworthiness, reliability, wisdom, and so on. Parents frequently get freaked at the changes that can occur during this "trust expedition" since things such as clothes, religion, music, hair, politics, and language can all be ruled largely by the trusted peer group during this stage—*though only for a while*. The important things that good parents quietly model—the values, the beliefs—can appear to have disappeared, but they are really just being tested out by the teen. They're still in there and usually reappear by mid- to late adolescence as the teen learns that trust need not be based on conformity with a peer group. (Good friends don't have to all think, act, and look the same.)

Autonomy is the asset where independence becomes all-important—independence from parental demands (for sure) but also independence from the peer group demands. Ironically this stage was first explored by your kid when he was about twenty-four months old. Remember the terrible twos? Well, here you go again. The teen conflicts that result from the fights against parental control can be disheartening, but less so if you pull back your lens to see that this is where your child is thinking critically and independently for himself. *This is a very good thing.* He may coldly reject your religion (or lack thereof) as dumb, but he might also reject his peers' drug use as dumber.

Initiative appears when your kid starts demanding (God forbid) to choose and pursue *her own* goals, apart from what *you* think she should do. When confronted by a teen demanding power (over a nonlethal choice), wise parents chant the following mantra again and again: *bad decisions made well (independently by the teen) teach much more than good decisions made poorly (forced by the parent)*; see "Decision Making" later in Part 9.

The storms of adolescence start to clear with the emergence of that final stage called **industry**, marked by that wonderful morning where your kid wakes up to the notion that he alone is responsible for doing the hard work required to accomplish his goals. That's right, dear parent, everything suddenly is no longer your fault. This is one of those great moments you've been working for all this time. Now he is finally ready to complete that task of identity formation.

If you take a step back from the daily struggles with your kid and look at her "crazy" behavior through the lens of these four steps, don't the conflicts begin to make a little more sense? And aren't you impressed with Mother Nature's blueprint for your kid? You should be, and impressed to the extent that you stay out of your child's way as much as safely possible so that she can more quickly navigate her way to adulthood. (See "Parenting Teenagers" later in Part 9.) The parental magic is in the balanced approach. Too much or too little parenting can delay your teen's graduation for years. Mother Nature really hates it when we screw around with her building plans.

WANT TO LEARN MORE?

The Adolescent: Development, Relationships, and Culture,
  twelfth edition, by F. Philip Rice and Kim Gale Dolgin (Allyn
  and Bacon, 2008)
Uncommon Sense for Parents with Teenagers, by Michael Riera
  (Celestial Arts, 2004)
Your Adolescent, by the American Academy of Child and Adolescent Psychiatry (HarperCollins, 2000)

Bribes/Incentives

"Never underestimate the effectiveness of a straight cash bribe."

—CLAUD COCKBURN

The best way to start the worst fight at a gathering of shrinks
is to ask the crowd whether bribing teens (using incentives) is a
good way to motivate them. The mere word *bribe* upsets many
experts since it implies paying someone to betray some moral/
ethical principle. Pro-bribery folks point out that emptying the
dishwasher or doing homework is not a betrayal of principle.
The anti-bribe folks answer that those behaviors are meaningless
if they're done for dollars rather than for values like learning,
caring, or responsibility. The pro crowd responds by saying that
all kids get bribed anyway, even the ones who don't get dollars,
since they know that cooperation does ultimately get them material and emotional rewards like cell phones and approval. The
con side then points to research showing that paying young kids
for grades worked only temporarily and then stopped when the
payoff was removed. The pro side sees that research as being too
limited in its scope and not incorporating the incentive switching
we'll discuss shortly.

The best answer about bribing effectiveness is *it depends*. If a kid can be motivated to do the right things for the right reasons without throwing money at her, that's certainly the best way to go. (See "Communication/Empathy" and "Parenting Teenagers" later in Part 9.) Talking and sharing feelings is always the best first course since that can tap your kid's "inside" or intrinsic motivation, which is always the most powerful. But if that better, higher-level approach constantly falls on deaf ears (while the teen's problems get worse and she loses critical ground in the game of life), then *well-designed* bribes can often cure that deafness and can actually help heal damaged relationships.

First, incentives can accomplish a couple of neat motivational tricks that punishments never can. Offering some payoff (versus taking stuff away) puts your child in the position of having *failed to earn a reward* instead of having a parent seize some beloved thing *that she already had*. The key difference is that when the child "fails to earn," she *hurts herself* instead of having a parent hurt her. Adolescent anger with oneself can be the start of psychological growth. Teenage fury with parents can arrest it.

A well-engineered bribe can also be a Trojan horse containing a surprise dose of ethical development hidden inside a material payoff. Kids who refuse to do the right thing for the right reason (responsibility) often find that doing the right thing for the *wrong* reason (a bribe) ambushes them with payoffs they never anticipated. They'll do the homework for the money and then get whacked with surprise rewards such as parental smiles, teacher praise, kudos from impressed friends, and a weird part deep inside of them that starts feeling good—*just for doing the right thing*. Over time the extrinsic payoff (money) can morph into an intrinsic reward (good feelings) that continues to motivate good behavior long after the bribe is forgotten. But this happens only *if* you slowly but immediately start to switch to those intrinsic reinforcers by praising the heck out of your kid when he makes an effort. And those new, good feelings can even heal that old, bad parent relationship to where talking and sharing starts to get things done without dollars.

Is bribing a miracle cure? Nope. When done well it might work half the time. But even if it fails, *it can succeed*. Because when a kid fails to do something to get something she wanted, she is now confronted with *her own* angering behavior, not her parents'. Reflecting about that failure can lead to learning that can get her a home run the next time she bats.

But be very careful about selecting bribery goals, and consider seeing a helper to guide you since this can get complex. For example, paying for great grades can buy you great cheating. And paying for dishwasher duty can have your kid demanding dollars for any request you might make. Wherever you can, reward more for sweaty efforts than for shiny As and more for widespread, mature behaviors (such as cooperation and respect) than for simple chores. Regardless of the task or goal, design your bribes to teach your kid that winning is defined not by her final score but by her playing as hard as she can.

WANT TO LEARN MORE?

Parenting Your Out-of-Control Teenager, by Scott Sells (St. Martin's Griffin, 2002)

Communication/Empathy

"I have found the best way to give advice to your children is to find out what they want and then advise them to do it."

—HARRY S. TRUMAN

"Give-'Em-Hell-Harry" made a great point about talking with kids, which explains why we parents get so frustrated in "communicating" with our adolescents. What we parents call "communication" is usually our "telling teens what to do." The irony is that telling teenagers what to do usually marks the end of communicating with them.

Effective communication is not advice giving but a linking of the minds of two people (contrary to the rumor, parents and kids are people too) in a respect-based dialogue where each freely expresses his thoughts and listens to those of the other. Listening is, however, not just hearing but hearing with a powerful tool called *empathy*. Empathy does not ask *if* what someone says makes sense but rather *how* what he says makes sense *to him*. That's an easy phrase to say and a tough philosophy to practice when your fourteen-year-old "communicates" that he feels suicidal or wants to go to a beer party. But lecturing him that suicide is stupid or yelling at his request for beer ends any chance you may have to equip him with thoughts that might protect him from the ten suicidal impulses and one hundred beer parties you'll never hear about. Listening quietly about why he feels as he does opens up the door to his thinking and allows you precious and rare access to impact that thinking—if and only if you teach your child about effective communication by doing it first. Here are a few pointers to help you:

DO

- View your teen's scary, angry, illogical thoughts/feelings as bad food—you want him to throw it all up (get it all out).
- Let your kid talk without interruption until he's finished.
- Restate what you hear him say and ask if you've got it right.
- Ask questions if you're not sure.
- Speak with respect for your teen's view, especially when that's insanely hard. ("I can see where going to that beer party is very important to you. You say that all of your

friends are going, that one kid's parents are providing the beer, and that you believe that alcohol can't really hurt you. Is that right?")

■ Respond only when your teen is finished and then only with your *thoughts*. ("Well, I'm afraid I see alcohol as deadly for teens. . . .") Your *decision* can come later. ("No, I'm sorry, but I can't allow you to go.")

■ Practice communicating when there's no big issue to talk about. (Make a habit of talking.)

DON'T

■ Interrupt to argue a point.

■ Discount what your teen is saying. ("This party can't be all that important.")

■ Give advice unless it's requested.

■ Argue about who's "right" but rather say that you see things differently.

A few other communication tips include timing (late at night works for teens), location (cars and coffee shops help), and style (calm and controlled is critical). Why all these rules about just talking with your kid? Because done well, effective communication is so much more than just trading words. It's the key to the heart of your child.

Want to Learn More

How to Talk So Teens Will Listen and Listen So Teens Will Talk, by Adele Faber and Elaine Mazlish (Collins, 2005)
Staying Connected to Your Teenager, by Michael Riera (Perseus Publishing, 2003)

Decision Making

"Of course I have goals. I just need to ask my parents what they are."

—BECKY, AGE FOURTEEN

A great paradox of parenting involves how we "teach" our kids to make good decisions by *making those good decisions for them.* This arrests the development of their ability to eventually function well on their own. Many of us parents sort of know this, but we keep on doing it anyway. We get so invested in our kids' immediate success (that A in algebra) that we fail to let them fail, which is often their first step toward learning how to succeed. We get so caught up in the *content* of our children's lives (such as grades) that we forget that our first job is to help them develop *processes* (decision-making skills, for example) that will lead them to define and pursue their own goals, a behavior also known as *maturity.*

The disquieting fact is that a bad decision made well (independently by the teen) teaches a lot more about decision making than a good decision made poorly (imposed by the parent). The proper parent role is to oversee adolescent decisions as a consultant and step in as a boss only when the stakes are very high. Understand that although you have to take the wheel of your teen's life at times ("No, you can't go to a beer party"), there will be no learning in those situations. Even in the life-threatening decisions, you must always look for ways to allow your kid the chance to make the right decision before you step in to take control as a last resort. The key to this approach is to be sure that kids handle the consequences of their decisions, good and bad— but that's another thing that we parents do poorly.

Every morning my son and I would have a screamer about whether or not he needed a coat for his walk to school. One fifteen-degree, forty-mile-an-hour-wind day I got smart and only suggested that he might need a coat over his T-shirt, a suggestion he promptly ridiculed. "OK," I said. Twenty minutes later a blue-hued kid crashed back through the door, grabbed his parka, and ran back out, yelling that he'd be home late from the detention he'd now have to serve for tardiness. Since then we've argued about a lot of things. We've never, ever argued about a coat.

That subzero chill factor is a great example of what's called a *natural consequence*, an outcome of a decision made by our teen that the world will hand to her. Our parent job is to quietly get out of the world's way whenever that consequence won't kill our kid since things such as windchills are terrific sources of learning. So are cops and teachers. But most cops and teachers have a hundred stories about overinvolved parents who fight judges and principals so that their little darlings don't have to suffer a reprimand in a courtroom or a D on a report card (even though both were clearly deserved). The kids, of course, are fine with this diplomatic immunity, blissfully unaware that all they're learning is how to phone home when the stuff hits the fan. Warren Zevon said this so well when he sang: "Send lawyers, guns, and money—Dad, get me out of this."

I know that my present successes are much more a product of my past failures than of my past successes. My triumphs I sort of remember. My failures I can recall in excruciating detail, so vividly that I remember daily never to do those dumb things again. If you think about it, might this be true for you as well? I believe it's true for your kid.

So as teens get smarter, smart parents get dumber. Whenever their adolescents ask, "What should I do about . . . ?" they shrug their shoulders and say, "Well, I really don't know. What do *you* think you should do?" If today you can bite your lip and allow your kid to make a lousy (non-life-threatening) decision, you might be laying the groundwork for a hundred better decisions tomorrow.

WANT TO LEARN MORE?

Ready or Not, Here Life Comes, by Mel Levine (Simon & Schuster, 2006)

Getting Help

"Mom, I don't think that holding hands with the shrink and chanting 'I am a worthy child of the cosmos' is going to help much."

—BAILEY, AGE SIXTEEN

I hate to be the bearer of bad news to worried parents, but getting good, expert help for your teen and/or family presents two new problems in addition to the one that brought you to this page. The first is getting your teen to think that seeing a helper might actually help. Teenagers are built by Mother Nature to *not* want adults in their lives. (See "Counseling, Refuses," Part 3.) Adolescence is a time when autonomy and independence become critical, when even thinking about going to see a shrink can feel like admitting defeat and becoming vulnerable to some weird, hippie doctor who will tell you that you're nuts. Many kids already suspect that they are nuts based on their normal but chaotic changes (see "Adolescent Brain Development," earlier in Part 9), and they worry that their secret will be out when they see Doctor Peaceandlove.

The second problem is that your kid might be right about the "weird, hippie doctor." The fact is that many of us shrinks *are* a tad weird, particularly when viewed through the very unforgiving, looking-for-a-reason-not-to-come-back lens of a teenage eye. Helpers who are good with adolescents are a rarer breed since, as you may have noticed, teens can sometimes be tough to talk with. So what to do?

First, approach your kid by saying that you are sure *you* could be doing things better to help him and the *family* needs to get some expert assistance to deal with the issue. Don't make your child feel as if he alone is the "crazy" one in the family. Share that distinction with him.

Next, limit the scope of his commitment to the process so he's less panicked about being trapped in endless therapy with some weirdo: "Let's see this helper a few times. If you really hate him, we'll find someone you do like." This helps the kid feel some power in this scary experience. Don't hesitate to offer an incentive if you must. That might get him over the hump of anticipatory resistance to that first session. Once he gets there, hopefully his fears will abate and he'll want to come back. The best way to ensure this outcome is by doing your homework and finding a good helper so that your kid's first session is not a disaster that leaves him vowing never to enter any neighborhood where a shrink resides. Start your search by chatting with as many teen-oriented folks as you can and asking them whom they would see for their own kid. Those referrers might be pediatricians, teachers, counselors, juvenile police officers, and so on. When one name pops up more than once, consider initially seeing that person alone to see if the shrink might "fit" well with your child.

Those helpers might have lots of different titles, such as *counselor, psychiatrist, psychologist, therapist,* or *social worker.* Those titles are far less important to you than are the recommendations of good people who know their stuff. The helping business works just like the parenting business: it's not about how many degrees we have; it's about what kind of relationship we can forge with a child. With a good, respect-based connection, wonderful things become possible. Without it, little is likely.

Identity

"Dad, that was last week that I was a pacifist vegan. Now I want to be a Marine."

I've always been fascinated by watching tough, sophisticated, and/or jaded adolescents get so excited over Halloween. Many teens rate that as their favorite holiday, a seemingly silly thing until you view it through the lens of adolescent development. In that frame, Halloween makes perfect sense.

That's because of how most experts define Mother Nature's mission statement for adolescence: *to figure out who we are.* Shrinks call this process *identity consolidation,* and most say this is the most critical task for your teenager, one far more important than his GPA or batting average. Because when you think about it, there is nothing more essential to the human experience than having things such as self-acceptance, values, beliefs, codes of conduct, and, most of all, some rationale to make all of the insanity somehow make sense, or at least be tolerable. With those things we are happy and productive. *We know who we are.* Without those things we are lost.

The rub is that those things are very different for each one of us. As far as I know, no one has yet created one set of identity factors that every one of us can accept. Like it or not, as a race we humans are more like a weird Halloween parade, a chaotic mass of competing, conflicting entities, each whole on her own but very different from her neighbor.

Your teenager is a nonstop trick-or-treater, constantly being influenced by other marchers and constantly experimenting and changing the colors and themes of her own costume (her identity). This process is fun when it's about dress-up, but it gets serious when it's about parenting, because the colors and themes (identity features) of teens usually differ from those of their parents, sometimes dramatically. By design, adolescents will "try on" a thousand different costumes of values, styles, beliefs, codes, and philosophies to see which ones fit and which ones seem stupid to them. That's nature's way of building identity. But the old Halloweeners often hate it when their teens think that their costume is better. That's when the fun parade of parenting can turn nasty.

Smart parents (usually the veterans who've made all the mistakes with their older kids) take a laid-back attitude toward these changes, supporting them as the all-important yet temporary experiments that they are and stepping in only when the stakes become life threatening. These parents have learned to pick battles knowing that interfering only turns what might have been a funny, two-day adventure (such as purple hair) into a yearlong war of attrition.

But if you can keep your cool and lovingly support your child's passing obsessions ("Yes, Sweetheart, maybe it would be great to be a monk in a mountaintop monastery in Mongolia"), the payoff is incredible. At the end of a long trail of some very weird costumes you will one day find a happy, confident, and productive young adult who loves you so much for being so understanding about Halloween.

Parenting Teenagers

"Before I got married I had six theories about bringing up children; now I have six children, and no theories."

— JOHN WILMOT

There is little in life that compares with parenting. Like ballet, it is one of those things that can look so simple and be so complex that it must be lived to be understood. Attempting to teach ballet or parenting in this short a format is crazy. But then again, I'm likely talking with a crazy parent here (stressed, exhausted, and worried), so here's a five-minute guide for your lifetime of parenting.

Job one is to define your mission, one that needs to be different from that of your parents. They lived in a world where it mostly worked to simply control children (which is usually not so hard to do). But given the brain challenges of adolescents and the insane world into which we've plunked them (see "Adolescent Brain Development" and "Adolescent Culture," earlier in Part 9), it is no longer safe only to control them. Today we must *teach our children to control themselves.*

Their culture is so powerful that it laughs at your attempts to keep it away from your teen. Think she's in a safe, drug-free school? The dealers do daily business in *most* high school homerooms in America. Keeping her focused on academics and sports to avoid risky sex? High-achieving girls are increasingly having cheap (and risky) sex as another form of "achievement." Emptying your home of alcohol so she won't drink? Booze is available at *most* of the teen parties she attends—and a third of the time it's *provided by the parents.* The growing list of cultural risks appears overwhelming, and it can be—if you fight this parenting war with the lessons from the last one.

Controlling is no longer the answer. *Teaching* is. Simply forcing your code of values and ethics on your teen because you "say so" won't get it done anymore. Today you must shape the *beliefs* of your child to help prepare her for the craziness that will get to her *no matter how vigilantly you police her and her world.* Teaching is not about lecturing or punishing. It's about building a respect-based connection with your kid and then endlessly chatting, quietly asking her questions to help *her* define *her* values before the madness comes knocking. Here are some parenting rules to help you get that done:

Connect with Respect

Before you can teach, you must connect in a respect-based relationship. True respect from a teen is an upward-looking admiration, a wanting to be like someone the teen sees as being better than he is. It is not based on fear. Contrary to the myth, adolescent boot camps clearly do not help kids become better. Although research absolutely proves this, we parents keep wondering if having big, scary men scream into the frightened faces of our nasty, disrespectful teenagers is the way to discipline them. Well, the answer depends on what you mean by discipline. Those techniques teach *fear*, not *respect*. Fear *will* buy you control—but only while you've got that 250-pound drill sergeant threatening your child. When he turns his back, the values and beliefs of your kid will again take over the reins of his behavior. Respect buys you the behavior you see *after* the drill sergeant is long gone. But true respect can only be earned, not demanded. So this means that we parents have to be better people than our kids if we're to earn their respect. Which brings up rule number two:

Be What You Want to See

Parental modeling is the most powerful way to shape a child's values (and thus her behavior). But before you ever get in a kid's face, first get in your own to take stock of what you're modeling for your teen. Want her to talk calmly and respectfully? How's your own temper? Want her to avoid drugs? How many beers are OK for you? If you are insulted by these questions, know the disquieting statistical fact that the only people in America indulging in more irresponsible behaviors than the teens are the *adults*. I "kid" you not. So before you do the "talk," check out your "walk."

Walk the Walk *and* Talk the Talk

Live your values, but don't forget to softly speak them as well. An amazing number of children report that they really don't know their parents' beliefs or values. So tell them, but be sure that the telling is a mutual sharing during ten thousand chats where your *questions about your child's opinions* make up most of the conversation. Research shows the most powerful tools that shrinks possess to change behaviors are *questions that lead to changes in the beliefs that drive those behaviors.* Those healing questions work only if you accept your child's beliefs without judgment or derision, *especially when you disagree with them.* We parents should softly share our own views only after we show acceptance of theirs: "Son, I agree with you when you say that it seems as if everyone around you drinks and that beer for sixteen-year-olds looks like no big deal. But I'm afraid that I see other related things that I'd like to share with you. . . ." If you're worried that disagreeing is a bad thing, check out rule number four:

Connect Through Loving Conflict

Remember childbirth? Was that a quiet, sweet, romantic adventure, or was pain, yelling, and a bit of blood involved? The reality is that childbirth is usually hard and often scary. And it's also an incredible miracle not to be missed. Life never gets more real. Well, as the parent of a teen, here you go again, except this time your child is breaking away from you psychologically. This is the "rebirth" of your child as a semiadult, another hard, scary, yet miraculous time.

Remember labor pains? That suffering provided the energy for a new life to break away from you. Conflict is the labor pain of adolescence, the energy for your aspiring adult to start to become her own person. In the right dose and in the right tone, conflict will help keep your kid safe (with conflict-causing limits) as well as help her define her own life-guiding values (by challenging yours with her own conflicting ideas).

The great irony of conflict done well is that it feels like *caring* to your child, even to the one who's screaming that you are ruining her life by not letting her go to Mexico on an unsupervised, coed trip. If you can *quietly* respond by saying that you love her too much to risk her getting hurt and that you love her enough to risk being hated by her, those calm statements will feel like loving safety fences, lifesaving limiters of behavior that she'll nevertheless fight to the death. But while she's fighting, she cannot help realizing that the permissive "cool" parents seem more invested in avoiding conflict than in the well-being of their kid. That's how conflict done well (without parental rage) can feel like caring to your teen, which is the prerequisite for connecting with her.

But don't expect her to tell you that, at least not for a decade or two. Expect her to be outraged and indignant and to occasionally violate your limits. That's just the wailing of the newly born. So . . .

Don't Fear Failure

Your teen's failures are your friends. You want your kid messing up while he's still under your roof so that you have a shot at helping him learn from his mistakes. Adolescent screwups are not catastrophes to be dreaded but windows of learning to be exploited. Caught him watching porn? *Finish watching it with him* and then insist on a conversation about the real lives of those screen people, along with requiring some research (perhaps a paper?) about the other impacts of porn on our culture. (See "Pornography, Watches" in Part 7.) Aghast at that thought? Well, I guarantee that so is he, a great "punishment" in itself. But also think about what that might accomplish versus grounding him for a week. The grounding will teach him that Mom is a witch and that porn costs one week's freedom. The talk might teach him that Mom is smarter than she looks and, even more important, that porn destroys lives. So when the stuff hits the fan . . .

Use Consequences, Not Punishments

Punishments are created to *hurt*. Consequences are crafted to *teach*. Punishments are groundings, take-aways of loved things, hurtings, and humiliations. These breed rage and dark dreams of paybacks. Consequences are restorations, amends, and humility. These breed learning:

I was literally in the midst of reading about consequences when the cops brought my daughter home. She was drinking with her friends and had vandalized some neighbors' properties. Two hours earlier I would have grounded her for six months, screamed at her for a day, and then let her out after a week of her driving me crazy. This time I sat up all night coming up with a consequence. The next day we retraced her drunken route, with her apologizing to each person she hurt and committing to restoring their damages—plus "interest" such as weeding their gardens. The last stop was at the police station, where she apologized to the arresting officers and then mopped out the cell and the car where she had vomited. The cops all nodded approvingly to each other and then to me as they watched her work. One told me it was unlikely they'd ever have to arrest my daughter again. On the ride home, my girl was dead silent. "Are you that furious with me?" I finally asked. "No" she answered. "I'm furious—with me."

And speaking of peace officers:

Be the Calm Cop with Your Kid

Ever get a ticket from an angry, sarcastic, and intimidating police officer: "Let me guess—your gas pedal got stuck, right?" He leaves you feeling outraged about his disrespectful behavior and justified about your own. You forget all about that stop sign that you ignored. A calm, respectful cop *who gives you the same ticket* achieves a very different end: "Sir, I'm afraid you missed that stop sign. Please slow down. We have terrible accidents here monthly. Better to get wherever late than not at all. I'll be back with your ticket as quickly as I can." The respectful cop leaves you *mad at you* and *at your driving behavior*, not at him.

Now think for a moment—which cop has the greater likelihood of shaping your beliefs, of impacting on your behavior *when no cop is around*? Think for another moment—which cop do you want to be with your kid? But before you become either cop . . .

Pick Your Battles

Picture three "in" baskets on your parenting desk. Basket three (the least critical) holds issues such as messy rooms, clothes (nonprovocative), hairstyles, and so on. These mean very little. I've known gangster-looking kids you'd cross the street to avoid who were straight-edgers (no sex or drugs). I've also met handsome kids in Izods and khakis (the ones you'd love your daughter to date) who dealt heroin. So don't waste invaluable parenting time on basket-three issues. Just sigh, smile, and then chalk these things up to harmless identity exploration. (See "Identity," earlier in Part 9.)

Basket two holds numbers such as GPAs and SATs. Beg, borrow, and bribe to get the best with these that you can, but don't get too crazy. Mother Nature has provided safety nets to handle problems such as messy rooms and mediocre grades. They're called gorgeous girlfriends ("EEEWWWW—you actually live like this?") and community colleges ("Since I screwed up high school, I'm learning how to study here, and then I'm transferring to State.") These nets help your child remedy basket-two issues later in life.

The truly important issues you'll find in basket one. These have to do with your kid's *heart*, his *values*, his *character*, and, most important of all, his *connection with you*. Without those assets he can spin off into deep space because there are no safety nets for the priority-one issues. This is why you must pull out all the stops when your kid's problems involve things such as compassion, honesty, commitment, loyalty, drugs, or violence. For when these basket-one assets are strong, everything else that matters eventually falls into place. But fixing basket-two and basket-three issues never fixes the things in basket one. Neat clothes do not build strong character, and groomed hair does not grow a great heart. So never risk a basket-one item by viciously fighting over something in basket two or three. Those are battles you might win in a war you will lose by breaking your connection with the heart of your child.

And whenever employing any of the preceding eight rules, be sure to . . .

Keep Your Cool

If you're sick of reading this suggestion, I'm really not sorry since this tip beyond all others works so great in parenting.

Have you ever noticed how easy it is to yell at someone who's yelling at you? That can actually feel good. Have you ever noticed how hard it is to yell at someone who answers you quietly and respectfully? It's like quicksand for the ego: the more you yell, the dumber you feel. And if not yelling over dumb stuff seems impossible to you, feel free to use my trick. Whenever I'm about to get in my kid's face and go King Kong over something stupid, I fast-forward in my head to that rapidly approaching day when I'm waving good-bye with a huge lump in my throat as she drives off to college or to the army. I ask myself how I will feel then about what I'm about to do now. I get real sober real quick. And if that trick fails, never forget to . . .

Apologize

Remember rules one and two? Perhaps the most powerful way you can model to your child *and* gain his respect is by apologizing. That simple exercise teaches wonderful lessons such as owning behavior, wrestling with imperfection, striving to be better—all those things that we can never preach into a child's head. Know that in the eyes of your child, you will never look bigger than when you make yourself small with an apology.

WANT TO LEARN MORE?

Positive Discipline for Teenagers, by Jane Nelsen and Lynn Lott (Three Rivers Press, 2000)

Staying Connected to Your Teenager: How to Keep Them Talking to You and How to Hear What They're Really Saying, by Michael Riera (Perseus Publishing, 2003)

Your Adolescent, by the American Academy of Child and Adolescent Psychiatry (HarperCollins, 1999)

Sexuality

It's still the same old story, a fight for love and glory . . . NOT!

If you're tempted to skip over this section because you were once a teen and know all there is to know about sex, then you are the parent who *most* needs to read this. I hate to break it to you, but a few things have changed in the world of teen sexuality.

The first is that if you believe that oral sex is sex (which many kids don't), then today's teens are having record levels of sex and at earlier-than-ever ages. The second change is that after years in decline, teen pregnancies and STDs have shot up again along with rates of sexual assault. The third bit of news is that the middle-school kids who are increasingly demanding and initiating casual "party" sex are . . . *the girls*. And that last headline might be the most startling of all.

The "old story" was that males were *physical*-sexual creatures, beings who could have casual sex and have little, if any, psychological/emotional fallout. To them, party sex was just an adventure. Females, it has long been believed, were *emotional*-sexual humans, people for whom healthy sexual function included cherishing, exclusivity, future planning, commitment—you know, all that "love" stuff.

In today's world the boys are pretty much same as they ever were. But many contemporary girls are now attempting to rewrite what most experts see as their innate female sexual wiring and instead trying to behave like the boys. Which raises a couple of key questions: Can they? And where is this coming from?

The "where from" question is easy—the culprit is their culture. (See "Adolescent Culture," earlier in Part 9.) Kids are being sexualized by the culture at very early ages and to degrees never before experienced by any other generation of children. The boys *and especially the girls* grow up defining themselves primarily as sexual creatures, beings who achieve worth by having sex. That credo works out better for the boys than for the girls, with the girls suffering dramatically. (Some things haven't changed.)

First, *even in this sexualized culture*, the girls often find themselves in a no-win position where they report that there are only two sexual labels for them: sluts or prudes. Boys who report (or lie about) being sexually active are "cool." While that may not be news, the recent cultural demand for children to be sexual makes that female label dilemma even more painful and ironic. Second, girls who attempt to sexually function like guys typically have higher-than-average rates of depression and anxiety. While experts argue the chicken-and-egg aspect of those numbers (did the behavior cause or follow the disorder?), you should also know that most girls express either regrets or conflicting feelings about having had casual sex. Most boys, of course, think party sex is just great.

Here's another worry. At those tender early-teen ages, kids are just beginning to develop true sexual identities, which include their values, codes of conduct, and sexual orientation. Developmentally, this is a very fluid and vulnerable time, when kids need to think and learn a lot about who they truly are *before* they embark on a defining course of sexual behavior. But our culture pushes them into "AP Sexuality" where at thirteen or fourteen they must declare themselves hetero-, homo-, or bisexual and are expected to have fully developed sexual codes to guide and protect them as they sexually engage each other. This is insane (and often damaging) for a couple of reasons. First, human sexuality is not a three-option choice but is actually a continuum of perhaps seven orientations that run from exclusive heterosexuality to exclusive homosexuality. The pick-one-of-three pressure is confusing. Second, by the time teens' true sexual identities begin to solidify, these kids are often in conflict with their prior behaviors. For example, girls who later decide that sex is a prized treasure to be shared only with faithful love partners sometimes can't reconcile that defining value with prior years of promiscuity, a conflict that might be related to those higher rates of depression and anxiety we see in girls who have casual sex. It's very hard to unring a bell.

What to do? Talk about sex. A lot. And early. (See "Communication/Empathy," earlier in Part 9.) We've now measured significant sexualization pressures on girls as young as age *four* (no, that's not a typo). "The Talk" should be ten thousand minitalks where you help the girls *and the boys* begin to see their over-the-edge sexual culture before it pushes them into behaviors for which they are not ready. For example, don't fast-forward through the sexual messages in the movies, but pause them and ask what your kids think about that stuff. If you worry that you're exposing them too early, know that you're probably too late. The average age of exposure to hard-core pornography in America is *ten*. And that pornography they see is not lovemaking; it's usually sadistic and misogynistic madness that I can't even describe here.

Dad, *you* should be the one to take your daughter out for a red-faced, stammering conversation at the coffee house about the sexual value differences between boys and girls. ("Yes, honey, some boys will lie to get sex. I know because I used to be a boy.") They'll believe you more than Mom because of your sexual credentials. And *Mom*, take your son out and use your own résumé to educate him about girls. ("Son, I know that some girls will approach you for casual sex, saying that it's fine for them. But as a woman I can tell you that girls are just not built that way, and when they do that stuff they hurt themselves, sometimes terribly. I have a question I'd like you not to answer but only to consider: are you willing to hurt a girl just to have some sex? Please think about it. It's important. Thanks for listening.")

And while I'm upsetting you, know that you've got to square up to the issues of sex education and contraception. It would be wonderful if abstinence-only programming worked. It doesn't, and the results of that experiment have been tragic for some of the kids whose parents hoped that it would. The safest sex education includes abstinence advice along with contraception information. No, that approach does not promote sexual activity if it's provided as a package from respected adults, especially from parents. Research shows that teaching inclusive sex ed delays sexual activity and decreases high-risk behaviors. Abstinence-only programming can sound great until your terrified, tearful daughter presents you with a positive pregnancy test.

There's another bell that can't be unrung.

WANT TO LEARN MORE?

Dilemmas of Desire: Teenaged Girls Talk About Sexuality, by Deborah L. Tolman (Harvard Press, 2005)

Unhooked: How Young Women Pursue Sex, Delay Love, and Lose at Both, by Laura Sessions Stepp (Riverhead Trade, 2008)

Your Adolescent, by the American Academy of Child and Adolescent Psychiatry (HarperCollins, 1999)

INDEX

ABOUT THE AUTHOR

DR. MICHAEL BRADLEY grew up in Philadelphia, where, as he says, he barely survived his own adolescence. Like so many teens, his path to his passion found many detours. He was an officer in the U.S. Army, a disc jockey, and a law school student before fate landed him in a job working with teenagers, a job he never dreamed he'd love. That experience caused him to switch his studies to psychology, eventually earning his doctorate from Temple University.

In the thirty years since, Dr. Bradley has worked with all kinds of teens in all kinds of places, including schools, prisons, and community programs. In addition to being a licensed clinical psychologist, Dr. Bradley holds a specialized certification in the treatment of substance abuse disorders and is a Diplomate and Fellow of the American Board of Forensic Examiners. His publications include numerous articles and three books: the bestselling *Yes, Your Teen IS Crazy: Loving Your Kid Without Losing Your Mind* (Harbor Press, 2003); *Yes, Your Parents ARE Crazy! A Teen Survival Guide* (Harbor Press, 2005); and *The Heart and Soul of the Next Generation* (Harbor Press, 2006).

He lives in suburban Philadelphia, where he worries constantly that his own two kids might turn out like him.

For speaking engagements, Dr. Bradley can be reached at his website at docmikebradley.com. Also be sure to check out his

Parent Forums section to see how thousands of other parents are pooling their wisdom to get their teens through these challenging times.

About the Illustrator

Daddy...What is NEPOTISM?

Ross Bradley is a 6′ Space Pirate who draws stuff for food sometimes. Between his father's beatings, Ross enjoys kittens, fireworks, messing with his dad, and any way of combining the three. When asked what it's like to be raised by a teen psychologist, Ross will usually set himself on fire.

AUTHOR'S NOTE: Ross (who created the cartoons in this book and his own bio above) is also my seventeen-year-old son, a young man of whom I could not be more proud. He'll be furious to know I told you this, but in addition to being an excellent student and a mediocre metal rock musician (his own rating) he constantly volunteers his time to help others (such as working with autistic children, and along with Pastors for Peace risking prosecution to transport badly needed medications to kids in Cuba who suffer as a result of the embargo). In short he is an incredible human being, one very different from me, and one much better than me.

I tell you all of this to note that while our family has had its share of "crazy" teen times as well, we have discovered firsthand that the philosophies that guide this book's parenting techniques actually work. As proof, I offer that Ross still speaks to me—mostly; although, after reading this, perhaps not.